LITERACY&
LEARNING
CENTERS™
FOR THE BIG KIDS

Building Literacy Skills and Content Knowledge for Grades 4–12

SECOND EDITION

Katherine S. McKnight, Ph.D.

Edited by Elaine Carlson
Front Cover design, layout and additional graphics by Kris Lantzy

Printed and bound in China

First Printing November 2019

Published by Engaging Learners, LLC
Antioch, IL

Visit EngagingLearners.com

For David, my husband,
who lovingly cheers me on.

For Ellie and Colin, my children,
who teach me lessons every day.

Praise for the Literacy & Learning Center Model

FROM THE EXPERTS

"Dr. McKnight has done it again! She made the case that the utilization of learning centers toward literacy development simply works, as evidenced via her **100% success rate in achieving academic gains** with her unique, centers-based approach."

Principal Baruti Kafele
Highly regarded author, speaker, urban educator and school transformer

"Katie McKnight's work is always grounded in two things: reality and research. The way she breaks sophisticated theory and research into **practical and doable steps for teachers translates into real results for students**. I have been learning for over a decade from McKnight and see how her flexible learning model translates into blended learning models, across grade levels, and into the practices of content area teachers in all kinds of districts."

Eileen Murphy
Founder & CEO of ThinkCERCA

"**Students deserve and need this kind of 'hands-on and minds-on' learning** to become more independent learners. Now is the time to diversify student experiences and let the lively sounds of activity ring out in your classroom."

Dr. Kathy Perez
Professor Emerita
Saint Mary's College of California, international consultant, author

"Not only does McKnight provide research to support how this way of teaching improves engagement and literacy among students, but she also produces action research from some of this nation's most struggling schools to demonstrate that **it works *quickly*!** Get your whole school on board and watch your literacy scores soar!"

LeAnn Nickelsen
Maximize Learning, Inc.
Atlanta, GA

"In the process of improving learning outcomes for students, one often hears that 'the joy has been removed from teaching.' Becoming adept at utilizing Literacy & Learning Centers in your classroom will **return the joy, raise test scores, and most importantly, increase student engagement**. Dr. McKnight has created a road map for Literacy & Learning Centers that is simple to follow but rich in results."

Julie Mitchell, MA, Ed. S.
Reading Specialist & School Advocate,
Resource Training & Solutions:
Regional Centers of Excellence
Central Lakes Region, MN

"This is for all the teachers who have questioned how to increase content-area literacy (while also keeping students motivated and engaged). Dr. McKnight's LLC model is **easy to implement in today's classrooms** and the activities provided are sure to keep the students engaged."

Melissa Dickson
Professional development presenter, teacher coach, and educator

FROM EDUCATORS LIKE YOU

"Once I started implementing Literacy & Learning Centers in my middle school science class, my students started becoming more engaged, showed immense growth and overall started to **deepen their understanding of content!**"

Cindy Nelson
Science teacher
Center for Educational Excellence
Tempe, AZ

"Dr. McKnight has found **the balance between content learning and the critical need for older students to develop their literacy skills.** The research-based Literacy & Learning Centers model allows for highly effective independent and small group center-based activities. You will want to start using centers in your classroom tomorrow."

Lisa Hollihan Allen
6-12 Literacy Intervention/Title 1
West De Pere School District, WI

"I'm really impressed. There was so much more [student] engagement! I'm feeling like **this is a game changer.**"

Stephanie Allen
7th grade ELA teacher
Kennewick, WA

"As center-based learning was implemented, an increase in student engagement, the use of best practices by teachers, and a **decrease in negative classroom behaviors** was observed."

Brenna Sherwood
Middle School Instructional Facilitator
Farmington Municipal Schools, Title 1
Farmington, NM

"I thought you might like to hear about the continuation of my growth using centers in the classroom, especially as I was one who doubted them up until the moment I used them. **The voodoo works.** My sped kids are getting it...my low kids are rocking it...and honestly, my job is 100X easier."

Allistare Lute
5th grade teacher
Indianapolis, IN

"As a high school reading teacher of many below grade level readers, I find it is sometimes difficult to find strategies to engage my students. Although my students can read, they often have difficulty connecting with texts in a meaningful way. **Literacy & Learning Centers have been a game-changer for my students,** not only in their interactions with texts, but by causing their reading comprehension and overall classroom achievement to increase exponentially!"

Elizabeth Knost
High School ELA teacher,
Anderson Community School Corporation
Anderson, IN

"Katie McKnight delivers **what all 21st century content-area teachers need** to be successful and confident in literacy development."

Elizabeth (Libby) Perry
Data/Literacy Coach
Anderson Elementary School
Anderson, IN

"McKnight's experience in using literacy centers to differentiate and teach important content is sure to **make an impact** on classrooms across the country."

Daniel M. Argentar
Communication Arts Instructor/Literacy Coach,
Adlai E. Stevenson High School
Lincolnshire, IL

ACKNOWLEDGMENTS

With all projects like writing a book, there are numerous people to thank and recognize. I would like to thank the many teachers who graciously allowed me to access their classrooms to co-teach, observe, and problem solve as we worked together to ensure that all children are engaged in dynamic and powerful learning.

Elaine Carlson, the goddess of all things administrative, is integral in all aspects of my professional work, including this book. If you call the Engaging Learners office, her pleasant demeanor is always on the other line. Kris Lantzy designed the cover, layout, graphics, and illustrations. I am lucky to know so many talented professionals.

ABOUT THE AUTHOR

Dr. Katherine McKnight is a dynamic presenter, dedicated teacher, and award-winning author. She began her career in education over 30 years ago as a middle school and high school English and social studies teacher in the Chicago Public Schools. In addition to speaking at professional development conferences, she is a regular consultant in schools and classrooms in the United States and Internationally.

Dr. McKnight has served as a Distinguished Professor of Research at National Louis University. She is the founder of Engaging Learners, an educational company built around her successful Literacy & Learning Center™ model. Her work in educational leadership, literacy and student skill development has resulted in unprecedented academic achievement in many struggling schools.

Katie has received several awards for her publications and teaching at the university level. She has authored 19 books that support educational strategies to engage all learners. Her titles include the best-selling *The Teacher's Big Book of Graphic Organizers (Grades 5-12)*, winner of the 2013 Teachers' Choice Award. She's also written *The Second City Guide to Improv in the Classroom; Teaching Writing in the Inclusive Classroom; The Elementary Teacher's Big Book of Graphic Organizers (Grades K-5); Literacy & Learning Centers: Content Area and Disciplinary Literacy Tools for Grades 4-12 (Volume 1);* and *Strategies to Support Struggling Adolescent Readers.*

TABLE OF CONTENTS

Chapter 1   **Why Should We Use Centers for the Big Kids?**, *page 9*

Chapter 2   **Getting Started**, *page 25*

Chapter 3   **The Foundational Centers: Teacher-Led Center, Vocabulary, Reading Together, and Writer's Craft**, *page 37*

Chapter 4   **Beyond the Foundational Centers**, *page 53*

Chapter 5   **Assessment in Literacy & Learning Centers**, *page 67*

Chapter 6   **Teacher Tips and Additional Advice**, *page 79*

Appendix A   **Selecting and Grouping Texts**, *page 85*

Appendix B   **Literacy & Learning Center Posters**, *page 125*

Appendix C   **Resources for Centers**, *page 159*

Appendix D   **Graphic Organizers and Handouts**, *page 165*
                 Vocabulary Slide, *page 168*
                 List-Group-Label, *page 169*
                 Cornell Notes, *page 170*
                 GIST, *page 171*
                 Evidence Based Written Argument, *page 172*
                 Panel of Experts, *page 173*
                 Sequence of Events, *page 174*
                 Story Trails, *page 175*
                 Commonly Used Prepositions, *page 176*

CHAPTER ONE

Why Should We Use Centers for the Big Kids?

CHAPTER ONE

Why Should We Use Centers for the Big Kids?

The Literacy & Learning Center™ (LLC) model is based on research and theory about the most effective practices for the development of literacy skills and content knowledge. LLC was developed through teacher collaboration that occurred in schools all over the United States and internationally.

As a veteran teacher myself, I am usually cautious when I am introduced to the "next great thing" in education. I know that a great teacher is dependent on many variables, including context, available resources, research, and most importantly, the diverse needs of students. Navigating the bridge that connects reading, writing and literacy skill development with content knowledge continues to challenge us. I have been working in this area for over thirty years and I will be the first to admit that I don't have the answers to all of the questions that face educators.

What I do have is a ton of ideas, and that is what this book and the LLC model are all about: ideas, creativity, effective research-based teaching, and ample practice. Since publication of the first edition, I have even more ideas and resources to share. When we bring together all of these principles, an effective model for the development of literacy skills and content knowledge emerges.

Frequently Asked Questions

Let me begin this chapter by addressing some frequently asked questions about using centers with older students. I am often asked:

ENGAGING™ LEARNERS

How can I teach literacy skills when I am required to cover content?

As educators, we need to resign ourselves to the reality that we will never, ever have enough time. That's just a fact. However, in the last decade, I have discovered that teachers, especially high school teachers, are very surprised when they realize that they are able to cover more content in less time through center-based instruction.

If our students are engaged in center-based activities, they are actually doing more, not less. When we lecture for what is sometimes referred to as "sit and get," our students become disengaged and bored. They aren't learning or retaining information.

After a year of using Literacy & Learning Centers™ in her classroom, Amy Kelley, a high school Spanish teacher observed, "I was hesitant at first but when I saw how engaged my students were when they worked in centers, the benefits became clear. Also, when my students' performances on exams were higher than ever before, I knew it was because of this instructional approach."

 Scan this code to hear more from Amy

Am I getting my students ready for college when I lecture?

In addition to being an experienced high school educator, I was a tenured professor for fifteen years at two different universities. Guess what? Long lectures that don't engage students are no longer the norm at most colleges and universities. Lecturing that does not allow for discussion and active interaction is not as effective as student-centered activities (Tovani & Moje, 2017). Furthermore, most colleges are preparing students for 21st century careers that require collaboration, creative problem solving and innovation. College assignments often call for completing portfolios, engaging in projects, and working as teams. Therefore, when high school students work in centers, they learn the skills that will be in demand in a college setting. They learn how to apply what they know and demonstrate their understanding of content.

How can I do centers if I have to get my students ready for "the test"?

This is largely connected to the first question. When I speak here of "the test," I refer to that high-stakes state assessment that exists in different versions throughout the country. Over the course of any school year, that test will produce anxiety for educators, schools, and students alike. Yet here's what I know: good teaching always takes care of testing. Always. When students are engaged in meaningful work in centers, and are actually doing rather than being lectured to, they learn how to be more independent, confident, knowledgeable and competent. In every district where I have implemented the Literacy & Learning Center model, student performance and proficiency has gone up. There's quite a bit of evidence out there, too, that if we keep purchasing test prep books and prepare students to take "the test," overall student performance goes down (Wilhelm et al.).

I have coached numerous schools where the Literacy & Learning Center model was implemented and student performance increased. For example:

Mesa View Middle School in Farmington, New Mexico was a Title I school that was struggling to raise performance. Over a two-year period, the Literacy & Learning Center model, coupled with a proficiency scale based assessment initiative, was implemented. In two years, Mesa View's state report card skyrocketed from an "F" school to a "B." Their sister school, Hermosa Middle School, witnessed similar gains. In the same two-year period, Hermosa's state report card rose from a "D" to a "B."

Here's another example. I served in an East St. Louis, Illinois district that had been featured in Jonathon Kozol's seminal work, *Savage Inequalities*. Mired in extreme poverty, the district was searching for new and innovative instructional methods for its students. For the first time in decades, after the introduction of the LLC model, the middle school and high school students in East St. Louis demonstrated increased performance on the Northwest Evaluation Association Measures of Academic Progress (NWEA) test. My East St. Louis colleagues and I were encouraged and excited to learn that the students' proficiency levels increased over 15% on the middle school and high school level in two years.

Why is the model called Literacy & Learning Centers rather than "stations?" What's the difference?

In elementary level classrooms, stations are generally characteristic of fixed, permanent locations for distinct instructional focuses. These stations might include a reading station on the rug, a listening station by the computer, and a writing station on the table by the window, for example. I deliberately chose the term Literacy & Learning Centers because, at the 4th–12th grade level, I wanted to imply that although students would move between focuses of instruction, the location and focus of the activities would be variable. For example, in a 9th grade Social Studies class the same "table by the window" might be used for a Reading Together Center, Writer's Craft Center, Vocabulary Center, map-interpretation, or graph analysis. The middle school and high school educational experience requires a model to be suitable for a wide range of content-areas and disciplines and infinitely malleable to accommodate the broad spectrum of skills and content knowledge that older students encounter.

Although there are subtle differences between the identifying terms, two important aspects of both models are that (1) new information and skills are delivered in small "chunks" so that students can easily process them, and (2) students are given ample opportunity to practice skills and process new information. This will be discussed in greater depth in Chapter 2.

To be honest, as an educator, I am reticent when someone shouts from the hilltop that they have THE answer for increasing student performance. I am immediately suspicious. It has been my experience that it is always a teacher, not a specific program that increases student achievement. For that reason, I ask only that you use this book as a resource and a guide. There is no one who knows his or her students better than a teacher. This book is intended to provide a model, tons of information, different sample activities, structures, suggestions, and teacher tips. I encourage you to treat the Literacy & Learning Center model as a guide. I expect you will make changes and adaptations according to your professional judgment.

The Literacy Challenge

National Assessment of Educational Progress (NAEP) data from 2013 indicates that over 60% of our high school students are not reading with proficiency. This means that our high school students lack the basic ability to read text for information, and therefore are not college and career ready (Bandeira de Mello, Bohrnstedt, Blankenship, & Sherman, 2015). In addition, more than 40% of college freshmen are required to take remedial courses before they begin work on their degree requirements (Chen, 2016).

I would argue that literacy is the critical foundation for all students to succeed. Yet, the dual priorities of building reading and writing skills while teaching content can be challenging for many teachers. When I became a high school teacher over thirty years ago, I was woefully unequipped to help students with reading difficulties. Unlike elementary school teachers, I was neither trained nor required to take any college courses in literacy when I prepared to become a teacher. Sadly, this is still the reality in many educational settings.

Richard Allington and Rachael Gabriel (2012) reported that there are six common factors that lead to school success and student growth. All six can be traced back to how students select their materials and practice their lessons as they develop literacy skills:

Six Common Factors That Lead to School Success and Student Growth

1. Every child reads something he or she chooses.

2. Every child reads accurately.

3. Every child reads something he or she understands.

4. Every child writes about something personally meaningful.

5. Every child talks with peers about reading and writing.

6. Every child listens to a fluent adult read aloud.

  ENGAGING™ LEARNERS

These factors are critical for academic success for students from every age group. The Literacy & Learning Center model embraces all of them – while also emphasizing the acquisition of content knowledge. Keep these six common factors in mind as you read through the following chapters. As you create Literacy & Learning Centers for your classroom, and adapt the model for your own students' needs, you'll want to keep coming back to this list. If your centers are built on these findings, then be assured that you are creating an awesome learning environment.

Five Components of Reading

As we continue to explore the Literacy Challenge, let's take a look at the five components of reading:

Five Essential Components of Reading

Phonemic Awareness

Phonemes are the smallest units that make up language. In English, there are 41 phonemes. When combined, phonemes create syllables and words. Phonemic awareness refers to the ability to identify and manipulate phonemes in spoken words.

Phonics

We call the predictable relationship between phonemes (spoken language) and graphemes (the letters and sounds in written language), phonics. Readers use these relationships to recognize familiar words and to decode unfamiliar ones.

Vocabulary

Students know and understand the meanings of words, and can use them with flexibility and precision.

Reading Fluency

Learners are able to identify words accurately and effortlessly, and read them within a text using appropriate intonation, stress and phrasing. We often assign fluency as an instructional focus for younger students but it is quite relevant for older students, especially as these readers encounter more complex, discipline specific text.

Comprehension

This is the process and product of constructing meaning from what we read. It consists of the interaction between a reader and a text, which occurs for a purpose and within a context.

What do the five components of reading mean for our older students, and how does this impact the teaching of our different content areas? Oftentimes, I encounter teachers who report that their students can decode text, but become puzzled when asked about the content of what they have read. Many of our students can decode and they "seem" to read, but they aren't able to make sense of the text. As teachers of adolescents, our students need us to primarily focus on comprehension skills and the development of academic- and content-specific language. If a student at this level (4th-12th grade) is still having difficulty with phonics, phonemic awareness, and fluency, they need the support of a reading interventionist. I often assert that it is completely unfair to expect a content area teacher to teach these skills. It is especially unfair to the struggling student. They need an expert who is trained in how to teach reading.

Comprehension and vocabulary should be the focus of all content specific teachers. As students progress through school, the demands of the texts they encounter increase. As Allington and Gabriel (2012) assert in their findings, students need practice and choice in order to develop greater skill proficiency. Jeff Wilhelm and Michael Smith arrived at similar conclusions about the importance of choice and practice (Wilhelm, Smith, & Fransen, 2014). This is exactly why tired practices like lectures, PowerPoints, round-robin reading, and all-class reading fail. During those ineffective exercises, students are not given the opportunity to demonstrate their understanding of content, and they are not allowed to exercise choice.

Let's Not Forget About Writing

Another challenge that faces many teachers is how to approach writing in the content areas and disciplines. In order for students to be college and career ready, they need ample writing practice, especially in evidence-based argumentation. In fact, argumentation is the heart of college and career readiness (Hillocks, Jr., 2011). Just as with reading, the Literacy & Learning Center model provides students the opportunity to practice their writing skill practice in all the content areas, even math.

Student Choice Doesn't Mean "Anything Goes"

Giving students a choice can sometimes make teachers nervous. This is part of why I refer to classroom choice as a "democratic dictatorship." I will offer my students choices, but they are always going to be choices that I provide. For example, let's say that students in a U.S. history class are studying the Bill of Rights. I want the students to write an evidence-based argument in response to the following prompt: "The Bill of Rights was written over two hundred years ago. Are these rights still relevant?" The students are instructed to choose one of the amendments and argue its relevance for 21st century America. The choice in this assignment is the opportunity for students to select any of the amendments that they wish.

Yes, incorporating student choice really can be this simple! Here's another example:

In a 7th grade English class, students are studying Edgar Allan Poe, with a focus on his impact on American literature and the short story genre. The students are offered the choice of reading any one of the following short stories: "The Tell-Tale Heart," "The Black Cat" or "The Cask of Amontillado." Regardless of which story they choose, students will develop the same literacy skills, and content instruction will focus on Poe's influence on the American short story genre.

We will continue to discuss the importance of student choice in subsequent chapters. Allowing students to pursue learning based on their personal interests is a great motivator, and it's an important component of the Literacy & Learning Center model.

More Reasons Why Centers Work for the Big Kids

There are several reasons why Literacy & Learning Centers are an effective strategy for developing content knowledge and literacy skills. The strategy aligns with several pedagogical approaches, including:

- Gradual Release of Responsibility
- Student Self-Regulation
- Formative Assessment
- Differentiated Instruction
- Multi-tiered System of Support (MTSS)

Gradual Release of Responsibility

The Gradual Release of Responsibility (GRR) model has been recently popularized as a result of the work of Fisher and Frey (2008), and due to college and career readiness standards that promote greater student independence. In short, this model promotes a three-step process. The teacher models an instructional strategy, the students practice this strategy with their peers, and then students grow into greater independence. In the Literacy & Learning Center model, GRR is the framework, or overarching paradigm. This is how the Literacy & Learning Center instructional model is aligned with GRR:

Gradual Release of Responsibility (GRR)	Literacy & Learning Centers (LLC)
I Do It	**Teacher-Led Mini-Lesson OR Whole Group Instruction** The teacher models a particular skill, usually through a think-aloud or read-aloud.
We Do It	**Pair/Small Group** In small groups, the students practice the skill that was demonstrated during the Teacher-Led Mini-Lesson/ Whole Group Instruction
You Do It	**Centers** The Literacy & Learning Centers include clearly focused activities that foster skill development and content knowledge.

The Literacy & Learning Center model shifts the focus of learning onto the student, while the teacher provides modeling and guidance through structured activities. When Literacy & Learning Centers are aligned with the GRR model, students can work toward developing a greater range of skills in order to promote independent learning.

ENGAGING™ LEARNERS

Student Self-Regulation

In many of the schools where I work, teachers and administrators report that their students often give up and do "just enough to get by." My colleague, Richard Cash, is an expert in student self-regulation. He and I have been fortunate to work in many different schools together. Lately, Dr. Cash and I have noticed that educators are recognizing the connections between self-regulation, growth mindset, and literacy development. We had the opportunity to test this connection for ourselves while working together at George Washington Community School in Indianapolis, Indiana, where we synchronized Cash's work in growth mindset with my work in literacy skill development and adolescent literacy.

According to Cash (2016), student self-regulation for learning and literacy develops within a cycle of learning, which can be identified as **Four Phases of Engaging in a Task** (see figure below). At first, a student must feel confident enough to pursue the tasks required. Then a plan to outline learning needs should be developed. This learning plan includes the *what*, *where* and *when* of the learning tasks. The third phase is self-monitoring, adjusting when necessary and reworking when needed. The final stage is the review and reflection stage. In this last step, the learner reviews what occurred, considers options for renewal or change, and sets a tone for the next learning task. Whenever a student progresses through the Four Phases of Engaging in a Task, he or she grows more confident and independent. This is essential for the process of literacy skill development.

Four Phases of Engaging in a Task

1) How well will I do?
Fostering Confidence

2) What will I do to do well?
Setting and Managing Goals

3) How well am I doing at doing well?
Monitoring and Adjusting

4) How well did I do at doing well?
Reviewing and Reflecting

Phase One: Fostering Confidence

Each phase of engaging in a task requires both self-regulatory strategies and literacy strategies. In phase one, students must find the mindset that will give them the best result. Carol S. Dweck (2006) describes the differences between a fixed mindset, where intelligence and ability are fixed and are unlikely to change, and a growth mindset, in which intelligence and ability can and will change with hard work and effort. Both types of mindsets are parts of living and learning, but we succeed by being able to shift to a growth mindset when it is necessary. In order to help students make that shift to a growth mindset, it is important to ensure they feel safe and welcome in their learning environments. Students who understand the expectations, norms and structures of their classrooms will be able to learn strategies to assist in these tasks (see figure below). Some ideas for fostering confidence in the classroom include:

- Creating and upholding the proper learning behaviors for the classroom

- Avoiding confrontations and power struggles in interacting with students

- Praising positive examples rather than singling out negative ones ("Ryan is working hard on his project!" rather than "Taylor, get to work.")

- Finding opportunities to reduce stress - after difficult tasks, take the time to play a game or tell a joke

- Not allowing students to "get your goat" - disagreements with students should be discussed one-on-one rather than in front of the class

AFFECT	BEHAVIOR	COGNITION
Safe & welcoming environment Building self-esteem & confidence Emotional resilience	Set scholarly expectations Develop academic habits, language Introduce the use of content language Actively uncover prior knowledge	Develop questioning strategies Build academic/ scholarly thinking Strategies to shift mindset

Sample Literacy Strategies
Read Aloud, Graphic Organizers, KWL/KIQ, Vocabulary Engagement/Instruction, Pre-Writing, Anticipatory Activities to Increase Interest, Word Sort/Trees, Brainstorming

 ENGAGING™ LEARNERS

Phase Two: Setting and Managing Goals

Next, students identify the plans and goals that will lead them to success. We can assist them in that endeavor by accentuating the worth and value in their aspirations. An ideal way to accomplish this is to cultivate student interest in the content. A student who wants to know more will feel more confident in setting a goal to achieve that knowledge. Additionally, students who witness teachers setting straightforward goals for upcoming work will know better what is expected of them. Students must also have the infra-cognitive thinking strategies readily available.

Goal setting is one great way to orient students for academic success. The acronym "SMART" helps students develop an action plan:

Specific: Select a clear target that you wish to improve upon.

Measurable: Define how you will measure your success.

Assignable: Plot out what materials, steps and resources you will need in order to succeed.

Relevant: Confirm that you have the resources available to complete your goal.

Time-bound: Determine a timeline for achieving your target.

AFFECT	BEHAVIOR	COGNITION
Encourage confidence through content awareness Manage stress, "boredom" and distractions Maintain a safe/risk-free environment	Learn study behaviors Develop organizational skills Maintain high expectations Teach goal setting Learn how to ask for help Learn to avoid distraction Strategies to overcome helplessness	Critical reasoning Essential question development and use Creative thinking HOTS (Higher Order Thinking Skills)

Sample Literacy Strategies
KWL/KIQ, Peer Assisted-Learning Strategies (PALS), Directed Reading and Thinking Activities (DRTA), Reader Response Journals, Note Taking Systems (Cornell), Structured Note Taking, Organizational Strategies, Graphic Organizers, Question Prompts, Concept Mapping, Brainstorming, Vocabulary Mapping, Formative Assessment

Phase Three: Monitoring and Adjusting

By this phase, students are ready to start assessing what learning strategies are and are not working for them. Monitoring and adjusting demands that students be fully aware of their own progress. A common way that this is done is through formative assessment strategies. Above all, quality formative assessments are descriptive. They tell students what they have accomplished as well as when and where they may want to change and improve their work. Descriptive feedback ought to have these qualities:

- Ongoing throughout the learning process
- Communicated to the student in a prompt manner
- Clearly related to skill and self-regulatory development
- Relevant to predetermined tasks, performances and goals
- Balanced, with neither too much nor too little detail
- Focused on students' effort, not their achievement

AFFECT	BEHAVIOR	COGNITION
Maintain confidence through success awareness Manage stress, "boredom" and distractions Maintain a safe/risk-free environment	Use and monitor study behaviors Use & monitor organizational skills Maintain high expectations Monitor goal approach Monitor assistance seeking Monitor distractions	Routinely using thinking tools Constructing essential questions and HOT (Higher Order Thinking) questions Implement creativity

Sample Literacy Strategies

Pre-assessment, Formative Assessment including Descriptive Feedback, Anticipation Guides, Entrance/Exit Slips, Question/Answer Relationships (QAR), Questioning the Author, Selective Highlighting, Marking Up the Text/Annotation, Reciprocal Teaching, Writing to Learn, Jigsaw, Frayer Model, Stop & Jot, Growth Mindset Questions

 ENGAGING™ LEARNERS

Phase Four: Reviewing and Reflecting

The educational philosopher John Dewey once said, "We learn more from the reflection on the experience than we do from the experience itself." So the fourth and final stage is a time for reflection. Students must identify what worked and why. They must also identify what didn't work and why. A cumulative assessment at this stage will demonstrate to learners how close to the learning goals they came, and how they effectively employed various strategies. By leading an in depth reflection, teachers can also help improve their students' capacity for meta-cognition and self-regulated learning during this phase. All this work is vital to cementing students' learning before they embark upon their next set of tasks.

There are many valid forms of reflection: journal entries, exit tickets, class discussions. Provide enough time for students to consider and record how they felt throughout each phase, what was successful and unsuccessful, and how they plan to improve in the future.

AFFECT	BEHAVIOR	COGNITION
Assess confidence through successes Assess stress, "boredom" and distractions levels Suggest environmental adaptations/adjustments	Assess study behaviors Assess organizational skills Assess meeting expectations Assess goal attainment	Reflection through meta-cognition Forecast mindset into the future

Sample Literacy Strategies
Summative Assessment Process, Reflection Logs, Portfolio Development, Collaborative Student Conversation, Teacher/Student Coaching Session, Summarizing (GIST), Graphic Representations of Learning, Goal Charting, Growth Mindset Compliments

This is how the Literacy & Learning Center instructional model is aligned with The Four Phases of Engaging in a Task:

The Four Steps of Engaging in a Task	Literacy & Learning Centers (LLC)
Phase One: Fostering Confidence	Mini-lessons provide students with models for literacy skill development in specific content areas and disciplines.
Phase Two: Setting and Managing Goals	Goal setting can occur during guided practice and/or when students are working with the teacher and peers at the Teacher-Led Center.
Phase Three: Monitoring and Adjusting	Students can monitor and adjust while working in collaborative centers, in the Teacher-Led Center, or at a designated Reflection Center.
Phase Four: Reviewing and Reflecting	Students have opportunities to reflect and revise while working in collaborative centers as well as in the Teacher-Led Center.

Formative Assessment

Developed through the work of James Popham (2006) and Margaret Heritage (2013), the Formative Assessment model provides an instructional approach to determining how and what students are learning. When teachers gain insight into their students via meaningful feedback, they are able to adjust instruction to ensure that their students are developing skills and acquiring necessary content knowledge. In addition, teachers provide meaningful feedback to students. Usually, this involves conferencing with students and providing on-the-spot, descriptive and supportive feedback. In classrooms that employ the Literacy & Learning Center model, students and teachers exchange feedback on a regular basis at the Teacher-Led Center. Here is a table relating the building blocks of formative assessment to the LLC model:

Building Block	Elements of the Building Block	Where this element is embedded in LLC Model
Learning Progressions	Learning progressions should clearly articulate the sub-goals of the ultimate learning goal.	Teacher-Led Center Proficiency scales
Learning Goals and Criteria for Success	Learning goals and criteria for success should be clearly identified and communicated to students.	Teacher-Led Center Each center has a clearly articulated focus. (See Chapter 2)
Descriptive Feedback	Students should be provided with evidence-based feedback that is linked to the intended instructional outcomes and criteria for success.	Teacher-Led Center Proficiency scales
Self- and Peer-Assessment	Both self- and peer-assessment are important for providing students an opportunity to think metacognitively about their learning.	Teacher-Led Center Working collaboratively in centers
Collaboration	A classroom culture in which teachers and students are partners in learning should be established.	As articulated in the Literacy & Learning Center expectations (see Chapter 3)

ENGAGING™ LEARNERS

We will discuss grading and assessment and how formative assessment is embedded within the Literacy & Learning Center model in greater depth later on in the book.

Differentiated Instruction

As I am writing this book, I realize that there is substantial misunderstanding about differentiated instruction. This is largely due to the fact that differentiated instruction covers many kinds of activities and types of instruction. To ensure that we all have the same definition, I want to outline what differentiated instruction is and is not. Rick Wormeli (2006) describes it as:

> Differentiated instruction is doing what's fair for students. It's a collection of best practices strategically employed to maximize students' learning at every turn, including giving them the tools to handle anything that is undifferentiated. It requires us to do different things for different students some, or a lot, of the time in order for them to learn when the general classroom approach does not meet students' needs. It is not individualized instruction, though that may happen from time to time as warranted. It's whatever works to advance the students. It's highly effective teaching. (p. 3)

Differentiated instruction within the Literacy & Learning Center model guides teachers and students to engage in the right instructional activities at the right time for the right purpose.

Specifically, Diane Heacox (2009) identifies twelve characteristics or elements of differentiated instruction (which, not coincidentally, are also compatible with formative assessment):

Twelve Characteristics of Differentiated Instruction

1. Integrate strategies for differentiation and Response to Intervention (RTI) in your classroom.

2. Identify Learning Goals

3. Examine your professional practices and skills in concert with your students' needs.

4. Apply practical, reliable and valid assessment strategies.

5. Create differentiated learning plans based on students' present needs.

6. Use choice to motivate your students.

7. Use flexible grouping for your students.

8. Be flexible in your teaching and responsive to your students' ongoing needs.

9. Develop student responsibility and independence in their learning.

10. Use ethical assessment practices that grow students (not punitive).

11. Differentiate learning for students with special needs and gifted students while incorporating learning profiles.

12. Create a teacher led leadership team as your school transitions to a differentiated instruction paradigm.

We know that all of our students are not the same. On the contrary, they are wonderfully unique. Yet, when we teachers are faced with large classes, how can we provide individual instruction and choice, as the differentiated instructional model promotes? The Literacy & Learning Center model is a teaching and learning method that meets these tenets of differentiated instruction. With Literacy & Learning Centers, teachers can create learning activities that involve student choice, flexible grouping, and modification of skills, the cornerstones of differentiated instruction.

Multi-Tiered Systems of Support (MTSS)

MTSS cannot work without a differentiated instructional approach. It is designed to identify struggling students before they fail and to provide immediate and targeted instruction to close achievement gaps with peers. Of course this is a brief explanation of MTSS. However, in the Literacy & Learning Center model, there is frequent and ongoing opportunity to work with struggling students and close achievement gaps. The Teacher-Led Center is the most critical component that allows this kind of intervention to occur.

Synergetic Approach

The Literacy & Learning Center instructional approach incorporates differentiated instruction, formative assessment, and response to intervention within a balanced literacy framework. When teachers plan instruction for this student-centered model, they find that they are better equipped to meet the needs of all students. The framework allows them to simultaneously develop literacy skills *and* content knowledge.

ENGAGING™ LEARNERS

Chapter References and Resources

Allington, R. L., & Gabriel, R. E. (2012). Every child, every day. *Educational Leadership*, 69(6), 10-15.

Bandeira de Mello, V., Bohrnstedt, G., Blankenship, C., & Sherman, D. (2015). *Mapping State Proficiency Standards onto NAEP Scales: Results from the 2013 NAEP Reading and Mathematics Assessments*. NCES 2015-046. National Center for Education Statistics.

Boekaerts, M., & Cascallar, E. (2006). How far have we moved toward the integration of theory and practice in self-regulation?. *Educational Psychology Review*, 18(3), 199-210.

Boekaerts, M., & Corno, L. (2005). Self-regulation in the classroom: A perspective on assessment and intervention. *Applied Psychology*, 54(2), 199-231.

Cash, R. M. (2010). *Advancing differentiation: Thinking and learning for the 21st century*. Minneapolis, MN: Free Spirit Publishing, Inc.

Cash, R. M. (2016). *Self-regulation in the classroom: Helping students learn how to learn*. Minneapolis, MN: Free Spirit Publishing, Inc.

Cash, R. M. (2016). Self-regulation for learning. In K.S. McKnight, (Ed.), *Addressing the needs of all learners in the era of changing standards: Helping our most vulnerable students succeed through teaching flexibility, innovation, and creativity* (31-52). Lanham, MD: Rowman & Littlefield.

Chen, X. (2016). Remedial Coursetaking at US Public 2-and 4-Year Institutions: Scope, Experiences, and Outcomes. Statistical Analysis Report. NCES 2016-405. National Center for Education Statistics.

Dweck, C. (2006). *Mindset: The new psychology of success*. New York, NY: Ballantine Books.

Fisher, D. B. & Frey, N. (2008). *Better learning through structured teaching: A framework for the gradual release of responsibility*. Alexandria, VA: Association for Supervision and Curriculum Development.

Heacox, D. (2009). *Making differentiation a habit: How to ensure success in academically diverse classrooms*. Minneapolis, MN: Free Spirit Publishing, Inc.

Heritage, M. (2013). *Formative assessment in practice: A process of inquiry and action*. Cambridge, MA: Harvard Education Press.

Hillocks, Jr., G. (2011). *Teaching argument writing, grades 6-12: Supporting claims with relevant evidence and clear reasoning*. Portsmouth, NH: Heinemann.

Kohn, L. Y. (2013). Engaging students to use their minds well: Exploring the relationship between critical thinking and formative assessment. *Inquiry: Critical Thinking Across the Disciplines*, 28(1), 36-45.

New Mexico Public Education Department. (2016). *New Mexico public school report cards*. Available from http://aae.ped.state.nm.us

Popham, W. J. (2006). *Defining and enhancing formative assessment*. University of California, Los Angeles, AfL Assessment for Learning.

Tovani, C., & Moje, E. B. (2017) No more telling as teaching: Less lecture, more engaged learning. Portsmouth, NH: Heinemann.

Wilhelm, J. D., Smith, M. W., & Fransen, S. (2014). *Reading unbound: Why kids need to read what they want—and why we should let them*. New York, NY: Scholastic.

Wormeli, R. (2006). *Fair isn't always equal: Assessing and grading in the differentiated classroom*. Portland, ME: Stenhouse.

Zimmerman, B.J., & Schunk, D.H. (2001). Reflections on theories of self-regulated learning and academic achievement. In B.J. Zimmerman & D.H. Schunk (Eds.), *Self-regulated learning and academic achievement: Theoretical perspectives* (2nd ed., pp. 273-292). Mahwah, NJ: Lawrence Erlbaum Associates.

Ready to introduce Literacy & Learning Centers in your school?

Need hands-on support?

Contact us at
info@EngagingLearners.com
or call **(312) 576-8222**

to schedule a free, no-obligation phone consultation with Dr. McKnight

The Engaging Learners team can come to YOU!

We work with school leadership to create customized professional development to address each school's unique challenges. Whether you're looking for a 1-day presentation, a hands-on workshop, or on-going support, our PD leaders will help your teachers achieve amazing literacy growth. Visit **www.EngagingLearners.com/on-site** for more info.

CHAPTER TWO

Getting Started

CHAPTER TWO

Getting Started

When students engage in focused, targeted activities in centers, they have opportunities to develop both their literacy skills and content knowledge. My work implementing learning centers has taken me to schools all over the United States. I have developed a model that has been used in content areas including English, social studies, science, foreign language, mathematics, vocational education, and even physical education. Teachers have also employed learning centers for Advanced Placement classes in numerous subjects.

One of the key factors of my Literacy & Learning Centers (LLC) model is that it is malleable. However, I want to be very clear that even though I recommend a specific approach, there is no one who is better equipped to analyze the needs of students than the teacher. If you need to tweak, adjust, or change the centers or the model, do it!

As you consider using centers for content teaching, I want to share how I implement Literacy & Learning Centers in the classroom. There are three specific segments of the model. The first segment is the mini-lesson, where the teacher introduces a new concept or skill to students. In this mini-lesson, the teacher models this concept or skill for students' benefit. The second segment is student practice. In this segment, the students practice that concept or skill that was introduced in the previous segment. Finally, the students transition to the center rotation. In the centers, students work to practice and refine skills and content knowledge. However, before we look at each individual segment, I want to discuss the importance of breaking down content knowledge and skill development into small, manageable pieces.

ENGAGING™
LEARNERS

Chunking Instruction

Specifically, chunking instructions is defined as the breaking down of content and skills into chunks that the brain can more easily process. Thanks to recent neuroscience research, we know that the working memory of the brain can manipulate only so much information at a time. Therefore, the brain prefers new information to be presented in distinct chunks.

As George Miller evidenced over 50 years ago (1956), our working memory has a limited capacity. He found that when a learner's working memory is full, the excess information is not retained. Think of a glass that you are filling with water. It has a limited capacity. If you were to keep filling the glass with water once capacity was reached, the excess would spill over and could not be contained in the glass. This is why, as teachers, we need to separate information into digestible chunks. This will serve to ease the reliable transference of concepts and skills into the working memory of the brain.

Literacy & Learning Centers provide a learning model in which students can process information related to newly acquired or developing skills. As we chunk new information for students, we ought to start with the most challenging. After these concepts are introduced, students should have ample opportunity to practice with this new information. Then, using Gradual Release of Responsibility (GRR) as a model, students will transition from observing to independently applying their new skills.

Step One: The Mini-Lesson (Teacher-Led Instruction)

Using the Gradual Release of Responsibility (GRR) model, effective Literacy & Learning Centers begin with a teacher-led lesson, or mini-lesson. You could introduce a skill or important content information for the students. Remember to chunk it!

Model skills for the students before they begin an activity, as the GRR model recommends. As we discussed in Chapter 1, the mini-lesson is the "I Do It" GRR component.

Here are some additional tips for the development of mini-lessons:

1. **Determine Content Need:** Perhaps you are a social studies teacher, about to begin a unit on the American Revolution. Before your students can begin studying documents from the period, they will need to develop the skill for sourcing documents. You might be a math teacher who needs to ensure that students have a thorough understanding of the difference between perimeter and circumference. To determine content need is to identify what skills and content are needed at each stage of an instructional unit.

2. **Keep Them Short:** Any mini-lesson that is more than 15 minutes is too long. Remember that we need to chunk information since the brain has a limited working memory.

3. **Make Them Simple:** Mini-lessons are most effective when concepts and skills are broken down into the most digestible chunks.

4. **Engage Students and Provide Interaction:** Now more than ever, we have to discover highly engaging and interesting instructional experiences for our technologically savvy students. Our 21st century students have unlimited access to information at any time. Consequently, classrooms must provide hands-on experiences that resemble the "real world."

5. **Provide Practice Time:** Before students are ready to implement newly acquired content knowledge and skills into their learning, they need practice. Build practice time into the mini-lessons.

6. **Consider "What's Next"?:** Perhaps your students have mastered the ability to identify and recognize figurative language like similes and metaphors in literature. Next, encourage them to use those literary devices in their own writing.

7. **Evaluate:** Determine and monitor if students are incorporating content and literacy skills into their academic work.

8. **As with all classroom activities, provide students with verbal *and* written directions.**

27

Step Two: Student Practice

This is an opportunity for students to work in pairs or possibly in small groups. During this time, the students have the opportunity to practice the skill or discuss the content that was introduced by the teacher in Step One: The Mini-Lesson. In the GRR framework, this is the "We Do It" component. The idea is to provide students enough practice time to develop skills and content knowledge. This is an integral factor for successful LLC, and it is especially important in light of Richard Allington's research (2012) about schools that are able to close the student achievement gap in literacy.

Practice is critical. Teachers often ask, "How long should students practice in Step Two?" I recommend about fifteen minutes for each center in this phase, but once again the teacher is always the best judge. Many students will benefit from slightly shorter practice sessions. With that said, and with what we know about the human attention span, aim for 15 minutes as the maximum practice time.

The latest neuroscience research has given us tremendous insight into our learning and brain development. As a result of this research, it has been determined that our attention span tends to be our chronological age multiplied by one. Therefore, if you are teaching 14-year-olds, their maximum attention span is 14 minutes (Statistic Brain 2016). One of the reasons why LLC is an effective instructional model is that activities are organized into developmentally appropriate chunks, which correspond to student attention spans.

Step Three: Center Time

Once the students have completed Steps One and Two, it's time for them to work in centers. No matter what your area of content expertise is, I always recommend starting with four foundational centers that we will examine in the next chapter. Once we discuss the four foundational centers, I will provide examples of additional centers for four major content areas: English language arts, social studies, science, and mathematics. For now, we will first examine how to group students and set up the centers.

Grouping Students

When I first taught in the late 1980s, cooperative learning was brand new. I was trained to group students heterogeneously and to consider factors such as ability, personality and work ethic. Students who might be shy were paired with gregarious students, and the more able students were placed with students who were still working on mastering skills and content. With the input of present day research, that conventional wisdom has changed a great deal. Specifically, we now know that grouping students based on ability, readiness and choice is more beneficial. Collaborative learning is preferred over cooperative learning.

Let's look at how cooperative and collaborative learning differ. Cooperative learning creates the expectation that the group members need to reach a consensus. There should be one answer or one product as a result of cooperation in the group. Collaborative learning is different. In a collaborative learning model, students prioritize discussion in order to share ideas and answers. It is acceptable for there to be more than one answer and approach, now that discussion and content exploration are primary goals.

Now let's consider how we group students. As we consider grouping students into temporary groups for different educational purposes, it is critical to note that this is not tracking. Tracking students usually locks them into one group or path. When we create temporary student groups for each instructional context, this is commonly referred to as flexible grouping. Students are grouped based on readiness, ability and choice in a flexible grouping model. One of the most important features of the LLC model is flexible grouping.

Ability Grouping is based on student performance. Most teachers use standardized testing data or measures like Lexile® to create these groups. Ability grouping is helpful when targeting a specific group of students for interventions.

Readiness Grouping is created in response to student performance. Are students ready to move to a new task or different level of instruction?

Choice Grouping is established through student's selection of a topic or text. Because students are grouped based on their choice, the groups are often composed of mixed ability members.

ENGAGING™
LEARNERS

Regardless of how you choose to create student groups, it is recommended that each group be comprised of three to five students.

Flexible grouping of students is optimal. Remember, flexible grouping is not synonymous with tracking. It's truly flexible. Rearranging and changing group composition depending on the task empowers us to better meet the diverse needs of our students.

The Truth About Student Choice

As we discussed in the previous chapter, there is a significant body of research that supports the positive correlation between increased student motivation and increased student choice. We know now that choice is a strong motivator for student learning. Furthermore, giving students a choice encourages them to learn from each other, and provides opportunities for them to draw on the individual strengths of classmates. There is also great value in allowing students to pursue learning based on their personal interests.

That being said, choice does not mean, "anything goes" in your classroom. To successfully incorporate this approach, allow students to select from a range of options that are supplied by the teacher.

Here are some additional examples of how student choice might work in an instructional context:

SCIENCE
8th grade

Ms. X. Ample's students are studying fungus. They are exploring the essential question, "How can fungus be beneficial or detrimental to an ecosystem?" Before the students begin their work in centers, Ms. X. Ample offers the students the opportunity to read and explore one of the following types of fungi: penicillin, zombie fungus, or toe fungus.

The students choose what they want to study and the groups are created based on their decision. (As you read this, you're probably already imagining which of your own students would choose to learn about toe fungus!)

MATHEMATICS
9th grade

Ms. X. Ample (she's quite versatile) reviewed the concepts of ratio and proportions during a mini-lesson. As she prepares her students to apply what they've learned in a center rotation, she asks them to select from one of the following:

Choice One: Based on what you understand about ratios and proportions, why are some goods sold in proportion while others are not? For example, flour and gasoline are sold by proportion but clothing and shoes are not.

Choice Two: Based on what you understand about ratios and proportions, determine how much time you will spend sleeping, eating, drinking, and watching TV in a lifetime.

The students are grouped based on their choice.

ENGLISH LANGUAGE ARTS
10th grade

Ms. X Ample's ELA students are reading *The Scarlet Letter* by Nathanial Hawthorne. As part of a chapters 13–15 review, students are asked to complete a graphic organizer to aid them in examining character traits and motivations of one of the following characters: Hester Prynne, Reverend Dimmesdale, or Roger Chillingworth.

The students are grouped based on their choice of character.

SOCIAL STUDIES
8th grade

Students are asked to examine primary source documents as part of a unit on the American Revolution. The aim of the exercise is to further their understanding of different groups' points of view during the period. The teacher, Ms. X. Ample, has already introduced the skill of "sourcing" a primary source document by using the Declaration of Independence as an example. The students are then given the following primary source documents from which to choose:

- George Washington's Commission as Commander-in-Chief (1775)

- Virginia Declaration of Rights (1776)

- Lee Resolution (1776)

The students choose the primary source that most interests them for further study in the center activities.

In each of the above examples, groups are formed based on students' choices. But notice that in each case, their instructor determined the options in advance. Therefore, the teacher remains the primary facilitator and guide for content knowledge development. The class members have simply been offered some independence in how they choose to engage with the subject matter.

Students exhibit more enthusiasm when they have a say in their activities or a choice in their reading materials. The more enthusiastic they are, the more likely they are to complete their assigned tasks. So whenever possible, give students a choice, even a small one, about how to execute an activity. Letting students choose between two or three texts about the same content, for example, yields great benefits. It is a significant step in the gradual release of responsibility that we all work toward in our classrooms.

Flexible Grouping's Connections to Text Complexity

When we offer students choices in their reading, we need to consider the entire text complexity model. Students will generally pick texts that they can understand. Oftentimes teachers will assign texts based on standardized test data. But that data relies generally on the quantitative measures of a text. This can be problematic because the text complexity model has three components that are synergistically equal. We know that students are more motivated to read challenging texts when they are given a choice. Let's take a close look at the text complexity model and how it impacts flexible grouping.

Text complexity consists of the following three components:

1. **Quantitative Measures.**
   These factors are difficult or impossible for a person to evaluate efficiently. They are typically measured by computer software. Examples include word length or frequency, sentence length, and text cohesion.

2. **Qualitative Dimensions.**
   These characteristics must be evaluated by a teacher. They include levels of meaning (for literary texts) or purpose (for informational texts), as well as structure, language conventionality and clarity, and knowledge demands.

3. **Reader and Task Considerations.**
   This component is best evaluated by a teacher who understands the students. It includes assessing the reader's motivation, knowledge, and experiences, as well as the purpose and complexity of a text.

Note that quantitative measures are only one-third of the total model for text complexity. The other two-thirds of the model requires the professional expertise of a teacher to determine if the text is challenging for a particular student. Students need to read a wide variety of texts that have been selected based on these three components. Assigning the ideal material will help them to develop literacy skills, comprehension, and close reading ability for college and career readiness. (Appendix A contains sample book lists that demonstrate the text complexity model on various subjects.)

The Nitty Gritty of Planning for Literacy & Learning Centers

If you're like me, you probably learned to plan your classes by dividing material into lessons that are based on a weekly calendar. I have discovered that this traditional model is not conducive to the Literacy & Learning Center (LLC) model. Instead, think of each chunk of instruction as a cycle that will extend over several days, periods or blocks. If you have students in a 90-minute block every day, then you may be able to finish the cycle in one day. If you have students for 45 minutes each day, a cycle could take several class periods over a number of days. As we prepare to look at the LLC cycle, keep the following in mind:

A Literacy & Learning Centers Cycle

- Consists of the following steps:

  Step One: mini-lesson
  Step Two: guided practice
  Step Three: centers

- Develops a clearly articulated set of learning goals and specific content knowledge

- Provides ample practice time

- Provides student choices, as appropriate

- Integrates formative assessment

In the following template, notice that each LLC cycle begins with an articulated goal and focus.

Literacy & Learning Center Cycle Planning Template

Topic	The **Topic** focuses on the specific skills in the LLC Cycle. Some examples might include: Narrative Text, Systems of Governments, Life Cycles, or Basic Equations.
Essential Questions	**Essential Questions** are BIG questions that require students to explore and reflect. They are not easily answered with one word or one sentence. Some examples might include: Why are some stories worth telling more than others? How do human beings impact the environment?
Teacher-Led Mini-Lesson or Whole Group Instruction	The **Mini-Lesson** is designed to introduce or review a particular skill or important content information. Mini-lessons should be 10-18 minutes long (depending on the grade level of the students) and the teacher should be modeling a skill for the students.
Pairs/Small Group activity	In **Small Groups** or **Pairs**, the students practice the skill that was introduced in the Mini-Lesson.
Center activities **Teacher-Led Center** **Vocabulary Center** **Reading Together Center** **Writer's Craft Center** (Additional centers that are based on content will be presented in Chapter 4.)	**Centers** give students an opportunity to practice their skills. Each center will provide students with a clearly articulated activity. The Teacher-Led Center provides students with small group instruction time with their teacher and also incorporates formative assessment and tiered interventions.

(Additional centers that are based on content will be presented in Chapter 4.)

Now that you have looked at the template Literacy & Learning Center cycle overview, I want to remind you of a few things. Although there are recommendations for the different centers, it is always up to the teacher to determine the activities for each center. There are four recommended foundational centers, which we will discuss in the next chapter. But if the students have significant reading to complete, you can create a LLC cycle in which two Reading Together Centers are included.

Here is a blank template for planning your own centers, as well as a few sample cycles from different content areas.

Literacy & Learning Center Cycle Planning Template

Topic:

Essential Question:

Teacher-Led Mini-Lesson or Whole Group Instruction:

Paired/Small Group Activity:

Center activities:

Teacher-Led Center:

Vocabulary Center:

Reading Together Center:

Writer's Craft Center:

7th Grade English Language Arts Sample:

Literacy & Learning Center Cycle Planning Template

Topic:

Analyzing figurative language in personal stories and literary text.

Essential Question:

How do words impact my personal stories and literary texts?

Teacher-Led Mini-Lesson or Whole Group Instruction:

The teacher will provide definitions and examples of the following figurative language devices: metaphor, simile and personification. Using a mentor text, the teacher identifies the figurative language devices. The students and teacher discuss how these devices impact the meaning of the text.

Paired/Small Group Activity:

In pairs, the students look at their previously assigned novel and identify samples of figurative language. The students discuss with their classmate in the small group setting how the figurative language impacts textual meaning.

Center activities:

Teacher-Led Center:

The teacher will check the students' responses from the paired/small group activity. If the students need more practice with the identification of figurative language devices and deeper analysis of how these devices function in text, the teacher will provide further practice at this center. For students who demonstrate that they have secured understanding of simile, metaphor and personification, further analysis and discussion can occur at this center.

Vocabulary Center:

Students will complete a conceptual exercise where they match personification, simile and metaphor to examples.

Reading Together Center:

Students will read a passage from their selected novel together. They should continue to identify and explain similes, metaphors and personification as appropriate.

Writer's Craft Center:

At this center, the students will write a summarization of their assigned novel while incorporating figurative language

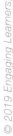

ENGAGING™
LEARNERS

6th Grade Science Class Sample:

Literacy & Learning Center Cycle Planning Template

Topic:
Exploring composers and decomposers in an ecosystem.
Essential Question:
Why do composers and decomposers keep an ecosystem healthy?
Teacher-Led Mini-Lesson or Whole Group Instruction:
Using visuals and video, the teacher will show examples of decompositions and explain why decomposition and composers contribute to the health of an ecosystem.
Paired/Small Group Activity:
In pairs, the students will examine an ecosystem and identify the composers and decomposers. They will be asked to elaborate on these identifications and justify their assertions concerning composers and decomposers.

Center activities:

Teacher-Led Center:

In the teacher-led center, the students will share their responses from the Paired/Small Group activity. The teacher will provide feedback to the students regarding their mastery of the presented concepts and record their responses for assessment purposes.

Vocabulary Center:

Once students have developed an in depth knowledge of the basic content, they are prepared to go further. Introduce additional related vocabulary and instruct the students to complete a graphic organizer for new terms.

Reading Together Center:

The students will select a scientific article about decomposition to read together. They will be instructed to identify the composers and decomposers in the ecosystem.

Writer's Craft Center:

Instruct the students to respond to the following claim based prompt:

Composers have a greater impact on the health of an ecosystem.
Decomposers have a greater impact on the health of an ecosystem.

Some Final Thoughts

When I work with fellow educators and share the Literacy & Learning Center model, the most common concerns are twofold. One worry is: "I don't think I have enough time to dedicate to Literacy & Learning Centers." Another: "I am worried that my students won't stay on task when I am working with students in small groups."

Here's my response to these real and legitimate concerns. Once teachers make the transition to Literacy & Learning Centers, they often report their surprise that they can actually cover more content in less time with their students. As I said in Chapter 1, we never, ever have enough time in schools and classrooms. However, we can work toward maximizing instruction within the allotted time. For the second concern about students staying on task during center time, colleagues often indicate how gratified they are to observe improvements in student focus through the LLC model. Students become more engaged, talk to each other, and commit to practicing newly acquired skills.

As teachers, we are innovators and creative professionals. In that spirit, I encourage you to read on.

 Scan this code to hear about Literacy & Learning Centers in the Classroom from Lyle, a 6th grade Language Arts Teacher

 Scan this code to hear about Literacy & Learning Centers in the Classroom from Laurie, a 6th-8th grade Vocal Music teacher

Chapter References and Resources

Allington, R. L., & Gabriel, R. E. (2012). Every child, every day. *Educational Leadership, 69*(6), 10-15.

Basar, E. (2016). *Memory and brain dynamics: Oscillations integrating attention, perception, learning, and memory*. Boca Raton, FL: CRC Press.

Beymer, P. N., & Thomson, M. M. (2015). The effects of choice in the classroom: Is there too little or too much choice? *Support for Learning*, 30(2). 105-120.

DuFour, R., & Marzano, R. J. (2015). *Leaders of learning: How district, school, and classroom leaders improve student achievement*. Bloomington, IN: Solution Tree Press.

Langer, E. J. (2016). *The power of mindful learning*. Boston, MA: Da Capo Press.

Miller, G. A. (1956). The magical number seven, plus or minus two: Some limits on our capacity for processing information. *Psychological Review* 63(2): 81-97.

Statistic Brain. (2016). *Attention span statistics* [Data set]. Retrieved from http://www.statisticbrain.com/attention-span-statistics

Wilhelm, J. D., Smith, M. W., & Fransen, S. (2014). *Reading unbound: Why kids need to read what they want—and why we should let them*. New York, NY: Scholastic.

CHAPTER THREE

The Foundational Centers: Teacher-Led Center,
Vocabulary, Reading Together, and Writer's Craft

CHAPTER THREE

The Foundational Centers: Teacher-Led Center, Vocabulary, Reading Together, and Writer's Craft

I recommend these four foundational centers since they are the concentrated source from which literacy skills are nurtured and developed. Students need ample practice in the areas that each center represents. Throughout this chapter, we will take a closer look at the four foundational centers: Teacher-Led Center, Vocabulary Center, Reading Together Center, and Writer's Craft Center.

Whether you're teaching ELA, social studies, science, humanities, or mathematics, I always recommend that the four foundational centers are included in a center rotation. After you've gotten comfortable with the model, however, there might be times you decide that you need to omit one or even replace one with a content-specific center of your own design. Remember, you are the instructional decision maker and no one knows your students better than you do.

Teacher-Led Center

In this center, students meet in a small group with their teacher. This is an excellent opportunity for teachers to provide descriptive feedback on student work. As we know from extensive research in assessment and grading (Heritage, 2010; Popham, 2005, 2011), providing immediate descriptive feedback about student work is critical for continued growth and achievement. Depending on the progress students have made, the teacher may use this center to provide support to students who need additional help, reinforce a particular skill for the benefit of the group, or provide enrichment opportunities to academically achieving students.

A proficiency scale offers teachers the framework to provide specific feedback to students. At Mesa View Middle School in

Farmington, NM a school that implemented Literacy & Learning Centers with great success, instructors use the Teacher-Led Center as an opportunity to discuss both simple and complex goals. Students display evidence of their developing mastery and share their work with their teachers.

Here's an example from Farmington's Proficiency Scales:

6th GRADE – LANGUAGE ARTS – Q3
Domain: The Art of Reading **Topic: Figurative Language**

4.0 I know all of the Simple and Complex Learning Goals and my understanding goes beyond the grade level target.

COMPLEX
3.0 I know all of the Simple and Complex Learning Goals.
- C1: Understand how specific word choice impacts mood (RL.6.4; RI.6.4)
- C2: Understand personification in context (L.6.5a)
- C3: Understand similies in context (L.6.5a)

2.5 I know all of the Simple Learning Goals and some of the Complex Learning Goals.

SIMPLE
2.0 I know all of the Simple Learning Goals.
Academic Vocabulary:
    V1: mood
    V2: personification
    V3: similie

    S1: Identify the mood of a passage
    S2: Identify personification in text
    S3: Identify similies in text

1.5 I know some of the Simple Learning Goals.
0.5 Not applicable
0.0 No evidence of knowing the Learning Goals.

In a proficiency scale, the goals begin at a basic understanding and mastery of skills, as articulated in the *Simple Goals* section. These targets then progress to more complex goals that require students to apply what they know and understand. Proficiency scales will be discussed in greater depth in Chapter 5.

Descriptive feedback is critical to the academic growth of students (Heritage 2005). For this feedback to be successful in the context of learning centers, it is important to bear several things in mind. To start, descriptive feedback is never in the form of a letter or numerical grade. Rather, it is a dialogue between you and the student. Where is the student mastering skills and content in their work? What does the student need to do in order to achieve higher levels of skill development?

How will the student attain greater understanding of the relevant content? This is where the continuum of skills laid out in the proficiency scale can prove useful in order to focus descriptive feedback.

As I work with teachers in schools, they express very legitimate concerns about having the time and ability to conference with every student. Providing individual descriptive feedback to each student seems overwhelming. I recall feeling similarly when I taught over 150 students each year. We will discuss descriptive feedback in greater detail in the assessment chapter, but in the meantime, let me offer some suggestions.

- Use the Teacher-Led Center as an opportunity to conference with students in either small groups or on an individual basis.

- Use proficiency scales and rubrics to focus on specific skills and content.

- When appropriate, students can also engage in peer feedback during collaborative work in centers.

Some Advice on the Teacher-Led Center

During the early stages of Literacy & Learning Center implementation, colleagues are often anxious about the Teacher-Led Center. The most frequent concern I hear is, "I am worried that the students won't stay on task if I am working with another group." Even in the most challenging classroom environments, it doesn't take long for the students to become increasingly independent and self-regulated. In order to guide students to work to a desired standard, it is important that teachers are consistent with expectations and norms for center work. Remember my earlier advice? You, as the teacher, are the best judge of what your students need in the classroom. If you want to transition to the Teacher-Led Center after the students have had some experience working in centers, then by all means, do so. However, don't wait too long, because the Teacher-Led Center is one of the keys to the LLC model.

Vocabulary Center

When I was a high school student over 30 years ago, I was often assigned long lists of vocabulary words and instructed to memorize them. I diligently wrote down each word three times along with its definition. Sometimes, I was required to write a sentence or paragraph using the new vocabulary words. Of course, I didn't retain much. We know now that this is actually the most ineffective way to teach because it creates a passive experience for students (Fisher & Frey 2014).

As students progress in their schooling, they delve more deeply into content-specific vocabulary. According to my colleagues, vocabulary, more than any other aspect of reading, presents the greatest challenge to student comprehension.

Every content area and discipline has specific vocabulary that students must learn. In the Vocabulary Center, students are given an opportunity to focus on activities that develop both academic and content-specific vocabulary. We are fortunate that substantial research (Marzano & Pickering, 2005; Coxhead, 2006; Fisher & Frey 2014) in this area provides the following recommendations for effective vocabulary instruction.

- Limit the number of vocabulary words to 12–15 per list.
- Give students an opportunity to practice with each new vocabulary word a minimum of five times in order to foster comprehension and usage.
- Teach vocabulary in context. To put it another way, students need to understand how words are connected. Providing long lists of vocabulary words that are not connected to current content area study is not an effective technique.

Students must be introduced to key academic vocabulary and given ample opportunities to practice new words as they develop content knowledge.

We know that having students copy words and definitions is the least successful way to teach new vocabulary. Yet, ironically, it remains the most common classroom strategy. We need to provide students with ample opportunities to work with language and new words.

Here are some examples of engaging activities that support vocabulary acquisition. All of these are well suited for use in the Vocabulary Center.

Vocabulary Chips

Vocabulary Chips develop students' understanding of synonyms, antonyms, and word relationships. Take some paint chips that you might find at a home improvement store. Using the different colors, students can take a root word and write antonyms or synonyms in the different shaded blocks. The students could also use the paint chips to represent associated words like: happy, joyous, delighted, or elated. Paint chips are also a useful tool for grouping related content-specific vocabulary words.

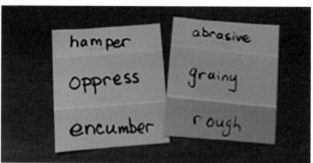

Vocabulary Chips Example

Vocabulary Chips Example

Vocabulary Jenga™

Vocabulary Jenga™ can help students review and further develop their understanding of newly introduced vocabulary. In this popular game, players pull out blocks from the tower. The object of the game is to remove blocks without toppling the tower. Elizabeth Knost, a teacher in Anderson, Indiana, uses this game as a Vocabulary Center. When each student removes a block from the tower, a vocabulary word is displayed. The student who removes the block has to explain what the vocabulary word means. If they are unable to do so, they have to remove another block.

Vocabulary Slides

Vocabulary Slides are a staple for language development. They are an effective way to graphically represent words and they prompt students to use new words and terminology. A sample of a **Vocabulary Slide** graphic organizer is on **PAGE 42**.

ENGAGING™ LEARNERS

List-Group-Label

The List-Group-Label activity encourages students to recognize relationships between words and concepts, and it helps them to understand and learn new vocabulary. The activity can be used before, during, or after reading. Directions:

1. Instruct the students to list all the words, phrases, and concepts they think are important in a text. Their word list can include new words as well as familiar words that are particularly important to the understanding of the text.

2. Direct students to work together as a team to group similar words together. They'll need to come up with at least three categories and decide where to put each word on their list.

3. When students finish grouping the words, instruct them to provide a written label for each group that reveals their reasoning.

A sample of a **List-Group-Label** graphic organizer is on **PAGE 43**.

Words That Are Confusing

Homonyms, or similarly sounding words, can be confusing. English language learners and native speakers alike often confuse these words in their writing, resulting in an incorrect word choice. This activity reinforces students' understanding of commonly confused words. It's a valuable addition to the ELA classroom but can be used any time a content-area teacher notices that students are confusing these words in their own writing. Before beginning the activity, write individual words from the confusing word pair list, on separate index cards and put them in a basket. Directions:

1. Instruct the students to dump the cards out of the basket and then work as a team to match them into their confusing word pairs or groups.

2. As a group, students should briefly discuss each group of confusing words. How do they differ in meaning? Do they sound exactly alike, or just similar? How might they remember which word to use in their own writing or speaking?

3. As a group, students should select one group or pair of confusing words and create an illustrated poster to help them remember the different meanings.

Confusing Word Pairs and Groups

board bored	break brake
capital capitol	choose chose
desert dessert	formally formerly
hear here	its it's
loose lose	quiet quite
peace piece	plain plane
principal principle	their there they're
theirs there's	to too two
threw through	waist waste
weather whether	who's whose

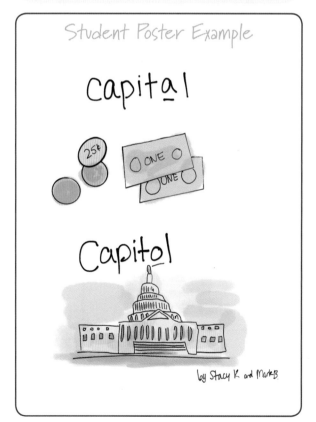

Student Poster Example

capital

Capitol

by Stacy K and Mark B

VOCABULARY SLIDE

Name: Sarah Brown

Date: 5/20/20

Synonym
Streamlined
Smooth

Picture or icon of vocabulary word

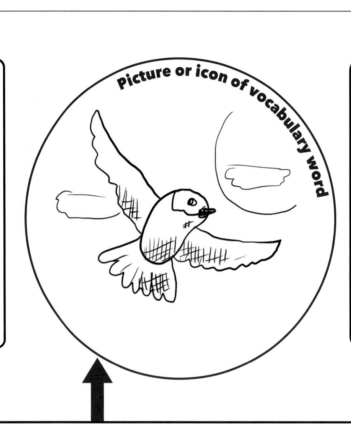

Antonymn
inefficient

Vocabulary word
aerodynamic

Part of speech
adjective

Sentence using the vocabulary word
Because it is aerodynamic, the airplane can stay in the sky.

  ENGAGING™ LEARNERS

See Appendix D for reproducible version.

LIST- GROUP- LABEL

Name: _Kenyon Battle_

Date: _3/13/20_

Write down the words, phrases, and concepts that were brainstormed. Include ones that you already knew.

establish justice

provide for common defense

promote general warfare

Constitution

United States of America

representative taxes

Speaker

officers

powers of impeachment

Preamble

Vice President

Categories

ROLES	PROTECTIONS	DOCUMENTS
Speakers	justice	Constitution
Officers	representative taxes	Preamble
Vice President	impeachment	

You have permission to reproduce this page for use in your classroom.

See Appendix D for reproducible version.

Some Advice on the Vocabulary Center

I am certain that you are already doing quite a few vocabulary activities with your students that can be developed into center activities. Use what you have and repackage it so that it will work as a focused center. Make sure that the information or skill you're teaching is a small enough "chunk" so that it fits into a five-minute mini-lesson. Another important piece of advice for the Vocabulary Center is the importance of visualization. Visualizing words and meanings is critical to internalizing new language (Hattie, 2012). As students progress in school, they will confront more and more terminology that is both high-level and discipline-specific. Therefore, it gets particularly challenging to internalize new vocabulary in the later grades. When students are advised to visualize new vocabulary, they are compelled to gain greater understanding of advanced meanings and concepts.

Reading Together Center

We know that once students develop skills in decoding and fluency, the simple act of reading more text improves comprehension. There are multiple research findings that show students are not reading enough in school (Wexler, 2018). As I've heard from colleagues, one of the biggest factors in this deficiency is that too many students are not motivated to read. There are solutions to this obstacle, however. Thanks to key reading researchers, we know that providing students with choices in their reading makes a big difference in motivation (Allington & Gabriel, 2012). Providing choice doesn't mean that students can select just any text. Choice means that we, as educators, provide two or more texts for students to choose from. In doing so, not only can we increase motivation, but we can also appeal to students of various interests and ability levels.

When we choose texts to offer our students, we need to provide a range of options and we need to rely on the text complexity model. Let's look at this in greater detail.

When students are offered a choice in what they are assigned to read, they are more enthusiastic about their work. By giving them some say over their reading material, it becomes more likely that they will complete those assignments.

This choice can, of course, be limited in scope, but it is important that students have some agency over what they read and how they approach an in-class activity. There are bound to be some exceptions to this model of student-selected texts, such as when a specific passage must be assigned in order for them to practice a particular skill. In most situations, however, allowing students a choice between several texts that all cover the same subject matter can bring about significant gains in productivity. Additionally, it will contribute to the gradual release of responsibility and greater student independence, a vital goal in any classroom.

As students will, after all, be reading together at this center, it is useful to consider how best to group students. A standard answer to this dilemma is to sort students by ability: below-level students read one text, at-level students read another, and above-level students read a third. In an even simpler approach, all student groups can read the same text, but they will read at varied speeds and with different levels of instructor support depending on their ability level. These are familiar approaches, but they are not the most effective ones.

I recommend that you group students not based on ability, but based on the texts they choose. Each student in the class will individually select the topic that most interests them, and will be placed in a group with the other students who picked the same text. This method of grouping provides a dramatic boost to student commitment and inspiration.

To reiterate, when students choose their reading assignment under this model, they are not simply selecting whatever they want. It is the teacher's responsibility to provide a range of text options for the classroom. For instance, if students are studying the Civil War in history class, offer five novels of differing themes and reading levels from which to

 ENGAGING™ LEARNERS

choose. Presenting a range of ideal options does require advanced preparation from the instructor, yes. There is a great reward, though, in that students of varied ability levels and interests all have an opportunity to engage with their reading.

Appendix A contains a selection of fictional and non-fictional texts that are suitable for use with the Literacy & Learning Center model. For each topic, the listed book suggestions cover a range of text complexities in order to serve students of varied reading ability.

As students grow older and engage with more discipline-specific material, their assigned texts grow increasingly complex. Reading together in centers gives them the opportunity to develop greater comprehension of this advanced content. Many of the strategies that you already use with your students can be easily adapted into centers. Here are some examples of activities that can be modeled in a mini-lesson and then included in a center rotation for additional practice.

The following activities are well suited for small group work in a Reading Together Center.

Sticky Notes

Sticky Notes is a strategy to develop the inner voice that all proficient and independent readers should possess. I always introduce the strategy in this way.

"When I am reading, there is a voice in my head. As I am reading, the voice in my head may ask questions about what I'm reading, make comments about what I'm reading, and draw personal connections with the text. As I read this text for you, I will stop whenever I have a question, comment or personal connection, record it on a sticky note, and place it in the text."

I demonstrate for the students how I think as a reader, and use sticky notes to develop my comprehension and understanding of the text. Once I model the sticky notes strategy, the students can use it when they are in the Reading Together Center.

A more detailed description of this strategy can be found in the next chapter, where you'll see how it can be applied in a content-area classroom.

Cornell Notes

Cornell Notes is a well-known comprehension strategy that encourages readers to dig deeply into a text and identify *main* ideas, concepts, or themes and separate them from *supporting* facts or details. Big ideas, called "Key Points," are recorded in the left-hand column, and the corresponding details and notes are recorded in the right-hand column. Students conclude the activity by writing a summary of the text.

A sample of a **Cornell Notes** graphic organizer is on PAGE 46.

Gist

Gist is an excellent activity to build comprehension and summarization skills. Here's how it works:

1. The students should preview an unfamiliar text. Instruct them to focus their attention to headings, sub-headings, and graphic elements like graphs, charts, and pictures.

2. Next, the students compile a list of words, phrases, and key vocabulary that they anticipate will be important for understanding the text.

3. Students read the text. Since they will have already previewed the text, they should have an effective guide to understand and better comprehend the content.

4. Finally, the students summarize the text in 20 words or less.

A sample of a **Gist** graphic organizer is on PAGE 47.

Some Advice on the Reading Together Center

Like with the Vocabulary Center, I have no doubt that you already have reading comprehension strategies and activities in your repertoire. For the Literacy & Learning Center model, use these strategies as mini-lessons or in a Teacher-Led Center prior to implementation of the small group activity. The students should see the strategy modeled and start out with some directed practice prior to using the strategy with greater independence in the Reading Together Center.

Remember that choice is the most effective way to group students and to motivate them to read. Students tend to pick books and texts that are "just right," and experience increased motivation and engagement when they are given the opportunity to do so. Also, don't forget that there is a rich book list that is organized by grade level, text complexity and essential questions and topics in Appendix A.

CORNELL NOTES

People in your Group: Jacob Steiner, Casey Feld, Mark Battle

Date: 3/10/20

Topic: Fables

Key Points:

The animals went hunting together.

The lion took all of the stag and shared none with the other animals.

Supporting Points/Details:

The Lion, Fox, Jackal and Wolf all went hunting for a stag together.

The Fox, Jackal and Wolf cut the stag in four parts and the lion took them all.

Summary:

Four animals went hunting together but the "greatest" animal is the only one who benefited. The other animals said that you can share work with the great but you won't share the rewards.

You have permission to reproduce this page for use in your classroom.

ENGAGING™ LEARNERS

See Appendix D for reproducible version.

GIST

People in your Group: <u>Charese Brown, Tia Barr, Susan William</u>

Date: <u>2/20/20</u>

Title of Reading Selection :

"Dorothy and the Wizard of Oz" by L. Frank Baum

Directions : Preview the reading selection. Write down the key words and phrases. Then write a 20-word summary sentence using as many of the keywords as you can.

Key words and phrases :

Land of Oz, Dorothy, the Wizard, Eureka the cat, Uncle Zeb, Emerald City, hot air balloon, magic powers, Glenda the Good Witch, Kansas, California, earthquake, horse and buggy carriage.

20-word summary sentence :

Dorothy leaves Kansas to visit her Uncle Zeb in California, they go to Oz in a balloon with a wizard.

You have permission to reproduce this page for use in your classroom.

Writer's Craft Center

In this center, students work on writing skills that are applicable to the content being studied. When looking for activities for the Writer's Craft Center, consider providing opportunities for students to practice skills that will be needed to produce longer texts. For example, students might complete a lab report for their science class. History students might use a graphic organizer to record primary source document evidence in support of a claim.

The following activities work well in a Writer's Craft Center.

Evidence Based Written Argumentation

Evidence based written argumentation is foundational for all areas of study. We use written argumentation in literary or historical analyses as well as science reports. It's everywhere in academic work and future careers. There are several ways in which we can develop written argumentation skills in the Writer's Craft Center. Here are some suggestions:

- Present students with a picture, photograph or video, and have them identify the claim and supporting evidence.

- Present students with a prompt and ask them to craft a written response that includes a claim and supporting evidence. (This longer-form writing will need to be completed over several Literacy & Learning Center cycles).

- Combine reading analysis with writing practice by providing students with a text and having them complete this graphic organizer.

A sample of an **Evidence Based Written Argument** graphic organizer is on **PAGE 49**.

Panel of Experts

Observers walking by your classroom door might think you've given your students the day off but you'll actually be engaging in an active learning activity that encourages them to develop oral communication, team building, self-awareness, self-confidence, critical and creative problem solving, and idea generation. In this exercise, a student group plays a Panel of Experts to answer questions from their teacher and classmates.

Directions:

1. Invite three to six players into the playing area. Players sit in chairs facing the 'audience' of remaining students.

2. The teacher assigns an area of expertise for each member on the panel. One traditional way to do this is to ask the audience simple questions and use their answers as the areas of expertise.

3. Ask each expert to introduce him/herself with a brief statement about his or her area of expertise.

4. The host (teacher) asks the panel questions and prompts each expert to answer in turn. Meanwhile, audience members record the panel's answers using a graphic organizer.

5. After the "interview" is complete, the class breaks up into small groups to discuss the points of view that they all heard in the Panel of Experts. Using their graphic organizers for reference, each student writes a summary from the perspective of the expert of their choice.

A sample of a **Panel of Experts** graphic organizer is on **PAGE 50**.

EVIDENCE BASED WRITTEN ARGUMENT

People in your Group: __Charlie Sciore, Hugh Garcia, Sara B. Clark__

Date: __4/21/2019__

What is the author's claim?:

Animals are smart.

What key points did the author use to support the claim?

Point #1
Pets react to human's moods.

Yes	No	
☒	☐	Does this point support the claim?
☒	☐	Is this point convincing/believable? Why or why not?

__Yes, Charlie's dog is quiet when Charlie feels sad.__

Point #2
Pets know when it is dinner time.

Yes	No	
☒	☐	Does this point support the claim?
☒	☐	Is this point convincing/believable? Why or why not?

__Yes, the author gave examples of dog's looking for food at 5pm.__

Point #3
Poison dart frogs have good memory skills.

Yes	No	
☒	☐	Does this point support the claim?
☒	☐	Is this point convincing/believable? Why or why not?

__The author said dart frog moms remember the locations of nests all over the jungle.__

What is this reader's conclusion?
Do you think the key points provide enough evidence to support the author's claim? Explain:

__We think the key points provide more than enough evidence to support the author's claim. The author showed us lots of evidence and facts that prove how smart animals are without a doubt.__

You have permission to reproduce this page for use in your classroom.

See Appendix D for reproducible version.

49

PANEL OF EXPERTS

People in your Group: __Charlie Sciore, Hugh Garcia, Sara B. Clark__

Date: __4/21/2019__

As you watch Panel of Experts, record the different points of view that are represented. Record corresponding details and information for each point of view. Use this information to draft a written summary of the presented information.

	Name of Expert	What is their viewpoint?	What details and evidence does the expert provide to support their viewpoint?
Expert One	Stacy	Frogs are the smartest animals.	Poison dart frogs remember all their nest's locations, frogs find shelter.
Expert Two	Mike	Bats don't need to see.	Bats use echolocation to find their way in the dark, so they don't need to see even though they aren't blind.
Expert Three	Emilia	Dolphins are great communicators.	Dolphins use clicks, echolocation and whistling to communicate with other dolphins and other animals.
Expert Four	Kim	Sharks don't need sleep.	Sharks can have restful periods, some always more, but they don't sleep to live like humans do!

You have permission to reproduce this page for use in your classroom.

  **ENGAGING™ LEARNERS**

See Appendix D for reproducible version.

Some Advice on the Writer's Craft Center

As with the other centers, the students should be engaging in clearly focused tasks. In other words, expecting students to write a full essay or composition is not realistic for a 15-minute center. Instead, have the students practice a specific skill or complete a step toward a larger writing assignment.

Students could:

- practice citing texts and sources
- identify reliable sources and evidence
- hone editing skills
- draft a segment from a larger composition

Like the other centers, the Writer's Craft Center is about providing students with the opportunity to practice skills so that they become more proficient.

Some Final Thoughts

As I have mentioned before, no one knows your students better than you do. Although I recommend these four foundational centers, only you can determine when you need to use them. As with all centers, ensure that you are creating focused tasks for your students that offer ample practice. Finally, remember that choice is a keen motivator for all students.

Chapter References and Resources

Allington, R. L., & Gabriel, R. E. (2012). Every child, every day. Educational Leadership, 69(6), 10-15.

Coxhead, A. (2006). *Essentials of teaching academic vocabulary*. Boston, MA: Houghton Mifflin Company.

Fisher, D., & Frey, N. (2014). Content area vocabulary learning. *The Reading Teacher*. 67(8), 594-599.

Hattie, J. (2012). Visible learning for teachers: *Maximizing impact on learning*. Abingdon, England: Routledge.

Heritage, M. (2010). *Formative assessment: Making it happen in the classroom*. Thousand Oaks, CA: Corwin Press.

Marzano, R. J., & Pickering, D. J. (2005). *Building academic vocabulary: Teacher's manual*. Alexandria, VA: Association for Supervision and Curriculum Development.

McKnight, K. S. (2010). *The teacher's big book of graphic organizers: 100 reproducible organizers that help kids with reading, writing, and the content areas*. San Francisco, CA: Jossey-Bass.

McKnight, K. S. (2014). *Common core literacy for ELA, history/social studies, and the humanities: Strategies to deepen content knowledge (grades 6-12)*. San Francisco, CA: Jossey-Bass.

Popham, W. J. (2005). *Classroom assessment: What teachers need to know (4th edition)*. Boston, MA: Pearson/Allyn and Bacon.

Popham, W. J. (2011). *Transformative assessment in action: An inside look at applying the process*. Alexandria, VA: Association for Supervision and Curriculum Development.

Wexler, M. (2018). Why American Students Haven't Gotten Better at Reading in 20 Years. [online] The Atlantic

Want more classroom activities?

Subscribe to
EngagingLearners.com/tools
for tools, teacher tips,
and classroom activities

The Literacy & Learning Centers Resources site is
your source for lessons that have been specifically
adapted to the Literacy & Learning Center model.

Try it FREE for two weeks!

Only $9.99/year for over 100 Literacy & Learning Center Activities and
Resources! Contact **info@engaginglearners.com** for details.

CHAPTER FOUR

Beyond the Foundational Centers

CHAPTER FOUR

Beyond the Foundational Centers

Beyond the four foundational centers that we discussed in the previous chapter, there are also centers that can be created for different content areas. This chapter will outline how to supplement the four foundational centers (Teacher-Led, Reading Together, Vocabulary and Writer's Craft) in English language arts, social studies, science and mathematics.

Please remember that you know your students better than anyone else, so I encourage you to adjust the model as you see fit. We will begin with English language arts.

Additional Centers for English Language Arts

Use Two Reading Together Centers

In addition to the Literacy & Learning Center model's four foundational centers, I suggest creating an additional Reading Together Center in ELA classrooms. It's usually a challenge for students to tackle the large volume of text that they encounter in this subject area, and ELA teachers need to provide them plenty of time to read.

Consider having one of the Reading Together Centers focus just on visualization as an effective means to develop comprehension. We know from the work of John Hattie (2008) and others that students develop greater comprehension and critical thinking skills after they can demonstrate what they know and understand visually. Many content literacy strategies, like the two that follow, require students to create visual depictions.

  ENGAGING™ LEARNERS

Identify and Illustrate Key Events

In this Literacy & Learning Center activity students visualize the answer to the following question, "What events do you think are most important from your reading and why?"

The phrasing for this question is important. Merely asking students to identify key events involves a lower level of critical thinking. After such an exercise, students will recall the key events but may not be able to explain why these are important. However, if students are required to pick which events they deem most important and explain why, it requires more analytical thinking. During the center activity, students will create a corresponding visualization of each event. This is an important step in the process of gaining greater comprehension. When students create a visual representation, they must engage in a critical analysis of the text that will propel greater understanding.

Story Trails/Sequencing

Many texts - both literature and informational - include sequential steps. To increase comprehension, give students an opportunity to practice identifying and visualizing the steps. ELA teachers may consider having students analyze a section of fiction or poetry that includes various plot points. Some passages that could work perfectly for this exercise include a chase scene or escalating confrontation. Directions:

1. Model the skill of identifying sequential steps for your students by offering a mini-lesson in identifying "clue words" like: *first, initially, next, then, eventually, meanwhile, so, finally,* etc.

2. Hang a poster or write center instructions similar to this:

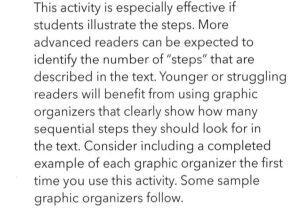

STORY TRAILS/SEQUENCING

IDENTIFY the suggested number of key events in the text. Be prepared to explain why you think each event is important.

CHOOSE one style of graphic organizer or use blank paper and create your own.

READ instructions on the graphic organizer. Look at a completed example if you need further explanation.

PUT important events in the correct order, completing the graphic organizer as instructed.

3. Provide various story trail or sequencing graphic organizers or blank paper for students who prefer to make their own. This activity is especially effective if students illustrate the steps. More advanced readers can be expected to identify the number of "steps" that are described in the text. Younger or struggling readers will benefit from using graphic organizers that clearly show how many sequential steps they should look for in the text. Consider including a completed example of each graphic organizer the first time you use this activity. Some sample graphic organizers follow.

Samples of **Story Trails/Sequence of Events** graphic organizers are on **PAGE 56 and 57**.

STORY TRAILS

People in your Group: <u>Kesha Clark, Lenese Andrews, Nathaniel Willett</u>

Date: <u>5/10/20</u>

1. Harry Potter meets Hagrid, and Hagrid tells him that he is a wizard.

2. Harry gets a wizarding wand in Diagon Alley.

3. The sorting hat places Harry in Gryffindor where he becomes friends with Ron and Hermione.

4. Harry gets the golden snitch and wins the Quidditch match.

5. Harry becomes a seeker on the Quidditch team.

6. Harry, Ron and Hermione defeat the troll and become suspicious of Professor Snape.

7. Harry finds out that Professor Quirrell is helping Lord Voldemort, with the Sorceror's Stone.

8. Harry destroys the Sorceror's stone.

9. Before the school year ends, Gryffindor wins the house cup. Everyone leaves for the summer vacation.

You have permission to reproduce this page for use in your classroom.

ENGAGING™
LEARNERS

See Appendix D for reproducible version.

SEQUENCE OF EVENTS

People in your Group: Anya Skinner, Parker Johnson

Date: 3/25/20

Event 1

In 1941, the US Army Corps (predecessor to the Air Force) was segregated. With WWII close, it was decided to offer training to African Americans as pilots and mechanics.

Event 2

The new air base at Tuskegee, Alabama, became the center for the training programs.

Event 3

First the 99th Fighter squadron and then the 332nd Fighter Group made contributions to the war efforts in North African and Sicily.

Event 4

The Tuskegee Airmen's pioneering contributions helped the subsequent drive to end racial segregation in the armed forces.

You have permission to reproduce this page for use in your classroom.

Grammar Center

In order to nurture students' English skills, I also recommend setting up a Grammar Center. At this center, students can work to develop their skills with academic language. Here's a sample of an activity that can be completed in the Grammar Center.

Placing Prepositions

When students understand how to identify and use prepositions, they become more skilled in adding spatial and temporal detail in writing and speaking. For this activity, you will need a small toy car and a small cutout of a person. Introduce the activity by demonstrating the relationship between the toy car and the cutout person. For example, the person can be "on top of the car," or "in the car." When you are done demonstrating the activity, put the car and cutout person at the Grammar Center for the students to use.

Directions:

1. Instruct the students to write as many statements, in the present tense, about the cutout person and the car. Give the students about five minutes to create and state as many relationships as possible between the cutout person and the toy car.

2. Next, give the students the handout list of common prepositions. Instruct the students to review the list and to identify how many prepositions they used.

3. In a large class discussion or in a Teacher-Led Center, discuss the value of prepositions in our language. Discuss how prepositions signal and introduce answers to the questions: *Where? When?* and *How?* Consider how they can change the meaning of a sentence.

COMMONLY USED PREPOSITIONS

aboard	about	above	across	after
against	along	amid	among	anti
around	as	at	before	behind
below	beneath	beside	besides	between
beyond	but	by	concerning	considering
despite	down	during	except	excepting
excluding	following	for	form	in
inside	into	like	minus	near
of	off	on	onto	opposite
outside	over	past	per	plus
regarding	round	save	since	then
through	to	toward	towards	under
underneath	unlike	until	up	upon
versus	via	with	within	without

See Appendix D for reproducible version.

Literary Terminology

Another topic that can benefit from this kind of specialized attention is literary terminology. At a center focused on terminology, students might work to achieve comprehensive understanding of a literary element. For example, figurative language devices such as similes and metaphors might be introduced in the mini-lesson. During the center rotation, you will have the opportunity to challenge students to apply what they learned about similes and metaphors to the text they are reading. This provides the students with an opportunity to practice, which will further their understanding of figurative language.

Speaking & Listening Center

A center devoted to developing student speaking and listening skills can be used in a variety of ways.

Read Alouds

Students have been shown to benefit from listening to a fluent adult read aloud (Skinner, Oliver, Hale, & Ziegler, 2006; Rasinski et al., 2005). So it is important to bear in mind that hearing a passage can be just as educationally valuable as reading it. Listening to a text is not cheating.

  ENGAGING™ LEARNERS

For example, listening to an authoritative adult reader can be a great way to introduce students to more complex works that they would be unable to read independently. English language learners profit from listening to a model English reader, and in particular, students with a reading disability can access texts that might otherwise be inaccessible. In order to help these lessons stick, encourage students to follow along in the written text while they are listening.

Small Group Discussion

Another option is to allow students to discuss their reading and writing. The Speaking & Listening Center can provide an opportunity for students to share thoughts and opinions about the assigned material as well as their own work with each other. We know from studies like Allington's (2012) that strong literacy programs are created where students have opportunities to discuss what they are reading and writing. This center can help clarify their interests and motivations for achievement.

More center activities for ELA classrooms are available at *EngagingLearners.com/tools.*

Additional Centers for Social Studies

Use Two Reading Together Centers

Like English language arts, social studies is a text-intensive discipline. Therefore, just like in an English class, I recommend two Reading Together Centers. By providing students with a second opportunity to delve into text, they can continue to hone comprehension skills and analysis. Remember that the students should practice strategies to develop comprehension skills. The Sticky Notes strategy that I introduced is an ideal way to put this practice into action:

Sticky Notes

One of the most effective ways to introduce the Sticky Notes activity is to project a text where everyone can see it. (Tip: Make it as large as you can so there will be room for the sticky notes.) Then, explain to the students that while you are reading, the voice in your head might ask questions about the text, remind you of something, or make a comment. Likewise, the words the author chose might cause your "inner eye" to visualize something. Tell the students that whenever you "hear" or "see" something, you're going to write or draw a reminder on a sticky note and put it on the part of the text that

inspired it. Don't be surprised if your students laugh. For some reason the idea of inner voices and inner eyes is very amusing. But don't let it throw you! I've found the activity can be just as effective when everyone is having some fun.

After describing the activity, model it. For example, imagine I was reading the following text aloud to a seventh grade classroom. I could pause at least 4 or 5 times to write sticky notes. Notice here that the notes don't have to be written in complete sentences. Take the time to reassure students that any messages they write as sticky notes are just for their own use; they don't have to make sense to anyone else, and everyone's will be different.

The Great Inka Road: Engineering an Empire
from the Smithsonian National Museum of the American Indian

The Inka called their empire Tawantinsuyu, **(Sticky note: sound it out?)** which means "the four regions together." **(Sticky note: Wonder what 4 regions?)** At its peak, **(Sticky note: Probably means when it was strongest)** the empire covered much of western South America. The Inka Empire rose rapidly and burned bright. **(Sticky note: Nice! Like a star!)** In little more than 100 years, it grew from a small kingdom in the highlands of Peru to become the largest empire in the Americas. **(Sticky note: 2 Continents)**

https://americanindian.si.edu/inkaroad/

After annotating the text, read it aloud without including the sticky note comments. Hearing the text through the voice of a confident reader will bring about new insights for your students. As they listen and follow along, their inner eyes and inner voices might even see and say some of the same things yours did.

Next, working together as a whole class or in small groups, repeat the activity with another short paragraph. Let the students brainstorm possible sticky note moments - those points where the text prompts their inner voices or inner eyes to say or see something. Finally, repeat the activity with a third paragraph, letting each student write his or her own sticky notes.

Try to work a version of this activity into your lessons at least once every week or so. You can apply it to your textbook or use supplemental material from websites, periodicals, or related trade books. Most importantly: encourage students to use sticky notes themselves, whenever they read independently. Watch their comprehension grow! See Appendix B for a poster you can recreate and hang in your classroom.

Here's an additional idea if you're looking to expand on the Sticky Note activity. It is designed to allow students to create and elaborate based on the observations of their inner voices. Ask students to choose one sticky note from their reading and write it out as a full sentence. Then, let pairs or small groups of students share their sentences. Rework the sentences as necessary until they all make sense, so students can practice refining their insight into a finished product. As a class, you can discuss how and why each reader has a unique reaction to a particular text.

Primary Source Center

Primary source documents are an integral part of the curriculum of many social studies courses. College and career readiness standards value a student's ability to analyze primary source documents and to cite evidence to support assertions and claims. A wide variety of primary sources are suitable for study in this center, including historical documents, journal accounts and artifacts. Hence, this is also an excellent opportunity to provide students with choices in their reading.

The following are some great resources for primary source documents:

Read Like a Historian (**https://sheg.stanford.edu**) is a free website that is sponsored by Stanford University. The website promotes student inquiry and analysis, using primary source documents as the focus and foundation for the development of critical thinking skills in history. With a free subscription, teachers will have access to lesson plans and resources.

Primary Source Sets, Library of Congress (www.loc.gov/teachers/classroommaterials/primarysourcesets) is a free site that groups primary source documents by subject and topic. The sources included are text based, visual and contain many oral histories. There are also teacher materials that include analysis tools for primary source study

Maps and Graphs Center

Non-text sources like maps, charts, and other visual documents make up a substantial portion of social studies content. The maps and graphs center provides an opportunity to study these sources in the context of the center rotation. The diversity of sources will deepen and enhance students' content comprehension.

Speaking & Listening Center
Multimedia

It is useful to have students listen to oral histories, music, or speeches from a historical context. This introduces audio content into the Literacy & Learning Center rotation, which can provide important background for the texts being studied.

The digital age offers many rich resources for further research in social studies. Using an abundance of online sources, students can view recorded historical events, detailed geographical maps, or newscasts. Through this center, they will take in and analyze information from these multimedia sources.

Sentence Starter Discussions

A Literacy & Learning Center activity like this encourages students to have authentic, engaging discussions, review content, and practice expressing clear thoughts using complete sentences. Unless they're already a regular part of your class routine, you might want to consider modeling sentence starters as a way to introduce this center activity. Students can also practice using sentence starters as part of whole-group discussion. Directions:

1. On colored index cards, write three claims about your study topic. These can be taken directly from a textbook or supplemental material – or you can make them up yourself.

Claim Card #1
Andrew Carnegie and John D. Rockefeller were robber barons because they exploited workers, built monopolies, and used their political connections to get rich.

Claim Card #2
The United States is currently experiencing a second Gilded Age.

Claim Card #3
The Gilded Age was a great period. It resulted in important food and medical regulation, technological developments, labor improvements, and social reforms.

  ENGAGING™ LEARNERS

2. On plain white index cards or strips of poster board, write sentence starters like these:

I agree with the claim because...
The point about...is important because...
I see it differently because...
This suggests that...
Despite agreeing with..., I disagree that ...
I agree, and...
An example of this is...
Put another way, the claim is stating...

3. Provide written activity instructions similar to these. Adapt them as necessary to suit your students and classroom needs:

AS A GROUP

1. Select a claim card for discussion.
Your group has two minutes to read each of the claim cards aloud and select one card for discussion

2. Discuss the claim.
Quickly select one sentence starter card each.

- Go around the table giving everyone a chance to say one sentence about the claim. Listen closely to what all of your groupmates say

- Swap your sentence starter card with another student

- Repeat the activity, this time using your new sentence starter card. Make sure you don't repeat what your groupmate said when he/she had that card. Say something new!

IF YOU HAVE TIME

Reflect. Take turns reflecting on the activity using one of the following questions as a prompt. Use your own words; you don't need sentence starters for this part of the activity!

- What one new thing did I learn during this conversation?

- Did I hear anything that made me see things in a new way or change my opinion?

- Did I express myself clearly? Did everyone understand me?

- Did I understand all my groupmates' sentences? (If not, ask him/her to re-state it or clarify it—and listen very closely this time.)

- If I could go back and say one of my sentences again, what would I change to make it clearer?

4. Keep those sentence starter cards and written activity instructions! You can use them over and over. Next time you do the activity you'll just have to change the claim cards to reflect your current topic.

Additional Centers for Science

Observation Center

Keen observation is a foundational skill for science students. This is true no matter which scientific discipline is being studied in the course. In a biology class, students could examine different items from the natural world through a microscope. As another example, in a physics class, students could work with magnets or experiment with kinesthetic models. Observation activities that are already a part of your curriculum can usually be adapted to the Literacy & Learning Center model with little effort. Consider this popular activity:

Why is it Like That?

This Literacy & Learning Center activity encourages students to rotate between centers as they apply scientific inquiry to answer a practical question. When they realize how methodical observations and reasoning can help answer real-life questions and solve small "mysteries," they will be better equipped to (1) apply similar logic to answer other questions, (2) appreciate how scientists discovered what we already know about the world, (3) realize how different scientists might reason differently and come to different conclusions, and (4) imagine themselves in the role of scientist.

The mini-lesson can focus on the importance of recording detailed and accurate observations, the value of logical reasoning, or the appropriate format for a scientific hypothesis. Adjust it according to your specific goals. Some teachers repeat the activity over the course of a few months, focusing on different steps each time. This activity often takes more than one center rotation to complete. Directions for this activity are on the following page.

1. To prepare the activity, write sentences identifying three or four "mysteries" that are readily observable in the school or classroom. For example:

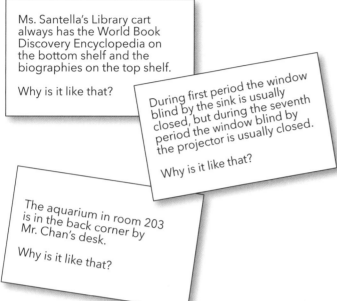

> Ms. Santella's Library cart always has the World Book Discovery Encyclopedia on the bottom shelf and the biographies on the top shelf.
>
> Why is it like that?

> During first period the window blind by the sink is usually closed, but during the seventh period the window blind by the projector is usually closed.
>
> Why is it like that?

> The aquarium in room 203 is in the back corner by Mr. Chan's desk.
>
> Why is it like that?

2. Let each group of students choose one mystery to work on.

3. To complete the Observation Center, instruct student teams to visit the site of the mystery and record three to five observations that might be relevant clues.

4. Students then return to a Speaking & Listening Center to discuss their observations and reasoning. Together, they decide on a most likely answer to the question.

5. Student teams work together in a Writer's Craft Center to write up their hypothesis. It's important that they clearly express their observations, describe their reasoning, and use proper grammar and vocabulary so that everything can be understood. They can move to a Grammar Center to proofread and edit their work if time permits.

6. After everyone has had an opportunity to solve a mystery, each hypothesis should be "peer reviewed" by the full class or in a Teacher-Led Center. Are the observations repeatable? Is the logic sound? Can the same observable facts be used to reach a different, equally reasonable conclusion?

Brenna, Maya, Joey, Stefan

Why is the aquarium in Rm 203 in the corner by Mr. Chan's desk?

What we observed:

1. The aquarium is about 12 feet away from the windows and about 20 feet away from the radiator.
2. There is about 3' between the aquarium and nearest furniture.
3. The sink is < 3' from the aquarium. There is 1 bucket and 2 syphon hoses in the sink
4. The aerator is plugged into the wall with no extension cord.
5. There are no dents in the floor so probably it has not been there a long time.

What we knew/believed before observing:

In the school paper (Sept.) there was a story about how some of Mr. Chan's Black Mollies died when the water got too hot.

Mr. Chan says he loves his fish so we believe he'd try to do the best thing.

How we could further our research:

We would like to see Mr. Chan clean the aquarium.

We could observe when the bell rang to see if anyone bumped the aquarium.

Our hypothesis:

The aquarium in room 203 is located in a convenient spot for cleaning, and it is out of the way of students and direct sunlight to keep the fish safe.

ENGAGING™ LEARNERS

Lab Center

Literacy & Learning Centers provide an ideal opportunity for students to practice special techniques that they will use in upcoming lab work. Skills such as taking precise measurements, observing the required safety precautions, and operating specialized equipment can be reinforced through a Lab Center.

Speaking & Listening Center

In this center, students can discuss different topics that have been introduced in class as they work to develop greater understanding.

Multimedia

Students can view online science resources from institutions like NASA, Scientific American™, or the Discovery Channel. A key component of science instruction is teaching students how to observe accurately and to draw appropriate conclusions from their observations. However, many important settings in science can be difficult to represent in a classroom during the school day. That is where this center can be a vital resource, in that students can go online to look at the night sky, space station views, deep sea scenes, life in a bee colony, and so on.

Dr. Know-It-All

In this activity, small groups of students work together as one mind – the mind of Dr. Know-It-All. Each student speaks one word at a time to communicate answers to audience questions. In addition to reviewing content, students develop skills in listening, oral communication, team building, self-confidence, and critical and creative problem solving.

Like most center activities, it is best to introduce Dr. Know-It-All as a mini-lesson. Once this is modeled for the students, they can complete the activity independently as a center activity.

Directions:

1. Set up three to eight chairs in a single row, facing forward, in the classroom playing area.

2. Invite teams of students to come forward and sit in the chairs to play Dr. Know-It-All.

3. The teacher acts as the moderator to field questions from the "audience."

4. Players answer the questions, each player giving just one word at a time.

5. Some answers may take the players two or more rounds to complete.

Use side-coaching to keep students on track. When students first learn this game, they may get distracted, argue with each other, and say things that don't make sense. Keep bringing their focus back to the question and what was already said. Typical side-coaching (things the instructor can expect to have to say during the activity) includes:

- "Listen to each other!"

- "Just say the next word!"

- "Remember, one word at a time!"

The instructor may also recap what has been said, or remind players of the question if they stall.

On the following page there is an example of what the Dr. Know-It-All activity typically sounds like in a classroom:

DR. KNOW-IT-ALL

Four students, Andy, Boaz, Dina, and Sabeeha are seated in chairs at the front of the class.

Teacher: We're very honored to have with us today Dr. Know-It-All, the world's leading expert on all things. Let's get a question for Dr. Know-It-All.

Student 1: (audience member): Dr. Know-It-All, how does a hurricane form?

Teacher: Ah, very interesting; what can you tell us about how hurricanes form, Dr. Know-It-All?

Andy: A

Boaz: hurricane

Dina: tries

Andy: Tries? That doesn't make sense.

Teacher: "A hurricane tries . . ." Go on, Sabeeha; see what you can do with that.

Sabeeha: hard.

Andy: I don't get it.

Teacher: A hurricane tries hard. . . .

Andy: to

Boaz: blow

Dina: down

Sabeeha: everything.

(Silence.)

Teacher: How does a hurricane form? Dr. Know-It-All tells us that, "A hurricane tries hard to blow down everything. . . ."

Andy: because!

Boaz: it

Dina: wants

Sabeeha: to

Andy: be important.

Teacher: Thank you, Dr. Know-It-All! Remember, one word at a time. Let's try another question; we've been studying hurricanes, so let's see if Dr. Know-It-All knows her facts – or if we can stump her!

Student 2: (audience member): What is the biggest danger when a hurricane approaches?

Andy: Storm

Boaz: surge

Dina: according

Sabeeha: to

Andy: weather

Boaz: experts.

 ENGAGING™ LEARNERS

Dr. Know-It-All, cont.

Here are some tips that have helped other teachers use the Dr. Know-It-All activity in their classrooms:

- The teacher can take a pretty firm hand as the moderator, making sense of crazy answers, steering the 'audience' toward specific questions, suggesting topics.

- As students become more familiar with the activity, they can take turns as the moderator.

- Some teachers might prefer to introduce this activity by practicing a whole-class version until students gain some familiarity with the one-word-at-a-time technique.

- If students are really struggling with speaking one word at a time, it's helpful to write down each individual word as it is spoken. Make sure you do so somewhere that the players can see them. This visual reinforcement is very useful for developing the language skills necessary for this game.

- Typically, the more specific the question, the shorter the answer.

- Especially as students are first learning the game, the teacher can modify the questions for the sake of simplicity and clarity.

- Allow students to make mistakes. They almost always do in the beginning. If allowed to make these mistakes, they will learn much faster than if the teacher or other students jump in to fix it.

This activity is an ideal way to review content using simple, knowledge-based questions. I've seen the Dr. Know-It-All activity used effectively in high school literature classes ("What metaphors are used to describe Pearl in *The Scarlet Letter*?"); ninth grade algebra ("How do you figure out the time traveled if you know the distance and speed?"); and second grade social studies ("What are the three basic human needs?").

"Dr. Know-It-All" activity © 2008 Katherine S. McKnight and Mary Scruggs from *The Second City Guide to Improv in the Classroom: Using Improvisation to Teach Skills and Boost Learning*

Additional Centers for Mathematics

Application Center

A comment that I often hear from mathematics teachers is that students are unable to generalize formulas and theories. Therefore, it is useful within the center rotation to demonstrate what sorts of problems and situations students can use each new formula to solve. In this center, students could be given problems where they need to apply mathematical skills, theorems, models, and postulates to different contexts.

Practice Center

Give students activities where they are practicing newly introduced material as well as previously presented material. Students need ample practice as they develop number sense and mathematical skills. Furthermore, working with topics out of new and old lessons side by side will help students absorb each new lesson into their comfort zones.

Some Final Thoughts

When students are offered clearly focused activities that include a range of choices, challenges, and practice activities, magic happens. The Literacy & Learning Centers model is built on key research-based instructional approaches that foster student growth and achievement (Gradual Release of Responsibility, balanced literacy, formative assessment, differentiated instruction, and multi-tiered intervention).

There is not *one* correct way to create centers for a specific content area. Focus on research-based practices that create positive and engaging learning experiences for students while keeping the following guidelines in mind:

- Create centers that provide students with ample opportunities to practice newly acquired skills and apply content knowledge.

- Chunk content into digestible pieces to facilitate scaffolding of new skills and content.

- Develop centers that adhere to what research indicates about attention span. Attention span is generally the chronological age of a student times one (i.e. 15 year-old sophomore x 1 = 15 minutes of focused attention).

- Be certain that students can work on each center activity independently

My final advice for this chapter is "Don't reinvent the wheel." Reflect on activities and instruction that you already have in your repertoire, and how to repackage those tools so as to meet the guidelines.

Chapter References and Resources

Allington, R. L., & Gabriel, R. E. (2012). Every child, every day. *Educational Leadership*, 69(6), 10-15.

Hattie, J. (2008). Visible learning: *A synthesis of over 800 meta-analyses relating to achievement.* Abingdon, England: Routledge.

Library of Congress. *Primary source sets*. Retrieved from http://www.loc.gov/teachers/classroommaterials/primarysourcesets/

McKnight, K. S. (2014). *Common core literacy for ELA, history/social studies, and the humanities: Strategies to deepen content knowledge (grades 6-12).* San Francisco, CA: Jossey-Bass.

McKnight, K. S. (2014). *Common core literacy for math, science, and technical subjects: Strategies to deepen content knowledge (grades 6–12).* San Francisco, CA: Jossey Bass.

Rasinski, T. V., Padak, N. D., McKeon, C. A., Wilfong, L. G., Friedauer, J. A., & Heim, P. (2005). Is reading fluency a key for successful high school reading? *Journal of Adolescent & Adult Literacy*, 49(1), 22-27.

Richardson, H. (2010, January 12.) Students only have '10-minute attention span.' *The BBC*. Retrieved from http://news.bbc.co.uk/2/hi/uk_news/education/8449307.stm

Stanford History Education Group. *Reading like a historian*. Retrieved from https://sheg.stanford.edu

Statistic Brain. (2016). *Attention span statistics*. Retrieved from http://www.statisticbrain.com/attention-span-statistics

Wilson, K. & Korn, J. H. (2007). Attention during lectures: Beyond ten minutes. *Teaching of Psychology*, 34(2), 85–89.

Winn, B. D., Skinner, C. H., Oliver, R., Hale, A. D., & Ziegler, M. (2006). The effects of listening while reading and repeated reading on the reading fluency of adult learners. *Journal of Adolescent and Adult Literacy*, 50(3), 196-205.

ENGAGING™ LEARNERS

CHAPTER FIVE
Assessment in Literacy & Learning Centers

CHAPTER FIVE

Assessment in Literacy & Learning Centers

When I discuss assessment with colleagues, the conversation often turns to the traditional grading system of A, B, C, D, and F. Sometimes I ask the question, "What are the criteria for earning each of these grades?" No one can reach a consensus—even within the same school, the same department, and the same grade level. As many educators reflect on their grading process, they invariably come to the realization that an A grade often indicates classroom compliance and consistent homework submission rather than a measurement of what individual students have learned or are able to do.

Much has been written about grades and what they mean for students. Although the grading system of A, B, C, D, and F has been around since long before we were in school, it's time to admit that these letters are not necessarily the most effective means of assessing our students.

Assessment is built on the premise that it should be reliable and fair (Wormeli, 2018). Our assessment tools should determine what a student knows and what they are able to do. Many educators argue that effective assessment should also aspire to measure skill development as well as student growth (Muñoz & Guskey, 2015; O'Connor, 2009). One of the strengths of the Literacy & Learning Centers (LLC) model is that it is built on the foundation of formative assessment, and is therefore well equipped to evaluate participating students.

We will now take the opportunity to examine formative assessment, and how it is oriented to measure student achievement in a way that provides more meaningful information about learning progress.

ENGAGING™ LEARNERS

What is Formative Assessment and How Does it Work in the LLC Instructional Model?

Let's start with a brief explanation of formative assessment before examining its role in contemporary education.

Formative assessment does not advocate one particular assessment strategy or technique. Instead, it refers to an ongoing process of gathering information about students' understanding. Using that information to its fullest potential can fine-tune your teaching and, as a result, enhance their learning opportunities. Foundational to this process is a feedback loop between teacher and student. This requires flexibility on the part of both participants. It is important that both sides of the loop understand that they are expected to make improvements since, just as a teacher can adjust instruction based on data gathered during formative assessment, so too can a student adjust his or her learning process. So it is important to note that formative assessment is a process, not a one-off effort.

The concept of formative assessment, as we think of it today, has been around for a while. In 1967, it was Michael Scriven who first explained how information gathered from evaluation could help formulate changes to a program and its corresponding teaching methods (Greenstein, 2010). Fast forward to just a few years ago, when states adopted new academic standards and various other state practices were introduced. Because most of these new standards focus on skill development, or what a student can do, rather than on simple information acquisition, formative assessment has emerged as a vitally important component of classroom education. Formative assessment is now widely accepted as ". . . a process used by teachers and students during instruction to improve students' achievement of intended instructional outcomes" (McManus, 2008).

Since every teaching and learning context can be different, formative assessment has many forms. And the most effective kind of formative assessment will incorporate a variety of tools and strategies that foster student growth and achievement.

Growth Mindset and Self-Regulated Learning

Before we get into the building blocks of formative assessment, I want to remind you again about the alignment between Literacy & Learning Centers, the pedagogical approach of self-regulated learning, and the important concept of growth mindset. I introduced this in Chapter 1, but there are a few more words about student growth and achievement that bear repeating.

As I write this book, a considerable amount of attention in education is being focused on the work of renowned psychologist Carol Dweck (2006). After decades of research, Dweck has come to believe that our mindset–how we feel about ourselves and how we learn–is closely tied to our achievement. She goes on to theorize that when we possess a growth mindset, we view challenges as exciting rather than as threatening (Dweck, 2014). For example, when a person with a growth mindset encounters a difficult task, she's likely to think, "Instead of fearing that this will reveal my weaknesses, I am going to seize the opportunity to grow."

All kinds of students benefit from this kind of mindset. Academically achieving and gifted students benefit because it frees them from the need to be perpetually reminded of how great they are. This mindset also eases the pressure of having to earn consistently high grades. It's empowering for them to focus on how much more they can achieve instead of focusing on maintaining status. Likewise, for our struggling students and for those who live in poverty, a growth mindset means they will get a welcome break from what may be perceived as a constant loop of negative feedback. Instead, they are encouraged to see how they can develop their skills and reach higher levels of achievement (Jensen, 2009). There are strong connections between growth mindset and literacy skill development.

The Building Blocks of Formative Assessment

So much of what happens in a well-functioning classroom exemplifies formative assessment. Every time a teacher alters a review activity to operate via a different instructional strategy so that a struggling student can grasp a concept, that's formative assessment in action. When students are encouraged to share what they already know about a particular topic before it's presented so the teacher can gauge how to introduce the material, that's formative assessment. Likewise, when a student self-reflects on a classroom activity, acknowledging when and/or if "a light bulb went on," that is formative assessment. (Moss & Brookhart 2019).

To the untrained eye, these examples may not look like they have anything in common. But formative assessment, especially as it is applied to the new standards-aligned classroom, has these distinct attributes.

Learning Progressions
Learning progression involves clearly articulating several sub-goals and relating them back to an ultimate learning goal.

Learning Goals and Criteria for Success
Learning goals and criteria for success should be clearly identified and communicated to students.

Descriptive Feedback
Students should be provided with evidence-based feedback after each activity. Be sure to explain how this input ties into success and the intended instructional outcome.

Collaboration
A classroom culture in which teachers and students are partners in learning should be established.

We'll examine these attributes one by one.

Learning Progressions

As students learn, their skills grow and they're able to grasp concepts of increasing complexity. In most state's academic standards, anchor standards for each grade level help signpost students' desired progression through their education.

Put simply, anchor standards represent the "big picture"– the goals that all students will strive toward in order to be considered college and career ready when they complete twelfth grade. The grade articulations are the steps along the way. Grade level articulations offer the teacher and learner clearly expressed short-term goals, and these short-term goals help in both lesson planning and assessment. It's important to recognize that most state's academic standards, whether anchor standards or grade level articulations, are student centered. That is, they are written from the students' perspective and they enunciate the students' goals. In other words, the teacher's job is to help each student achieve the goal. The standards are not goals for the teacher to achieve.

In other words, academic standards articulate how students ought to progress in skill development by the time they graduate from high school. Each of these standards is then articulated into grade levels. Let's take this reading anchor standard: "[The student can] read closely to determine what the text says explicitly and to make logical inferences from it; cite specific textual evidence when writing or speaking to support conclusions drawn from the text." Examine how this anchor standard is broken into the following learning progressions (*right*).

Now that standards for student achievement have been formulated, we can return to our discussion of formative assessment. In this context, formative assessment then refers to the methods everyone—both teachers and students—can use to determine what skills a student has at any given moment, what skills they are expected to have, and what the difference is between the two.

Learning Goals and Criteria for Success

It stands to reason that students are unlikely to achieve goals that aren't clearly articulated. Everyone wants students to be "better writers," for example. But what does that mean? What exactly is good writing? How will a student know whether an assignment she has completed fits that definition? How will the teacher know?

It's imperative that a teacher be able to define learning goals, to give students the necessary tools to achieve the goals, and to allow time and opportunity for practice along the way. (Scriffiny, 2008). Effective formative assessment requires the teacher to confirm that each student understands exactly what is expected of him or her. The criteria must be communicated clearly and in language the students can understand. And the students, in turn, need to confirm their understanding of the goal. This will determine the nature of the instruction and practice that follows. If mutual understanding has not been achieved, the work students complete may not necessarily contribute to their positive development.

The learning goals and success criteria take place at the lesson level. These are referred to as the learning goals or lesson objectives. If we take the example of the learning progressions, the grade level articulations exemplified in the previous section must be broken down even further into a learning goal or objective. These are commonly found in daily lesson plans. The following example illustrates the breakdown of learning progressions and grade level articulations into learning goals.

	[The student can] read closely to determine what the text says explicitly and to make logical inferences from it; cite specific textual evidence when writing or speaking to support conclusions drawn from the text.	
Grade Level	**Learning Progression** (Grade Level Articulation)	**Learning Goals (or Objectives)**
5th Grade	Quote accurately from a text when explaining what the text says explicitly and when drawing inferences from the text.	Quote text accurately and use proper punctuation. Identifies what the text explicitly says. Able to draw textual inferences.
6th Grade	Cite textual evidence to support analysis of what the text says explicitly as well as inferences drawn from the text.	Cite textual evidence using MLA or APA format. Cite textual evidence using MLA or APA format in support of textual evidence. Accurately cites evidence. Uses inferences to draw deeper contextual meaning of text.
7th Grade	Cite several pieces of textual evidence to support analysis of what the text says explicitly as well as inferences drawn from the text.	Cites several pieces of textual evidence using MLA or APA format. Cites explicit textual evidence using MLA or APA format as support. Accurately cites evidence. Uses inferences to draw deeper contextual meaning of text.
8th Grade	Cite the textual evidence that most strongly supports an analysis of what the text says explicitly as well as inferences drawn from the text.	Distinguishes between text evidence and selects what most strongly supports an analysis. Cites several pieces of textual evidence using MLA or APA format. Uses inferences to draw deeper contextual meaning out of text.
9th-10th Grade	Cite strong and thorough textual evidence to support analysis of what the text says explicitly as well as inferences drawn from the text.	Makes judgments about strength of textual evidence for analysis. Selects strongest evidence to support analysis. Uses inferences to draw deeper contextual meaning of text and is able to apply to analysis.
11th-12th Grade	Cite strong and thorough textual evidence to support analysis of what the text says explicitly as well as inferences drawn from the text, including determining where the text leaves matters uncertain.	Selects strongest evidence to support analysis. Uses inferences to draw deeper contextual meaning of text and is able to apply to analysis. Develops and applies additional textual support when the text leaves matters uncertain.

Descriptive Feedback

Formative assessment demands that teachers provide timely, specific feedback to each student. It is not sufficient just to compare his or her work with the work of other students or measure it against a predetermined "average." However, descriptive feedback is most effective when it compares an individual's work to a predefined learning goal. Remember, the point of formative assessment is not to rank or compare students; it is to compare each student's skills to the skills articulated in the goal.

Some teachers encourage students to ask themselves three questions during the descriptive feedback phase of formative assessment:

- Where am I going?

- Where am I now?

- How can I close the gap?

Descriptive feedback can happen at any time. In fact, it often happens repeatedly and spontaneously. Feedback that happens while the student is working is often the most effective. And, as with learning goals, feedback must be communicated clearly, in language the students can understand. The Teacher-Led Center in the Literacy & Learning Centers instructional model provides an excellent opportunity for consistent descriptive feedback.

Here's what a descriptive feedback session in a Teacher-Led Center might sound like:

Ms. X. Ample and four students are at the Teacher-Led Center.

Ms. X. Ample: I would like you to take out your Writer's Craft activity from yesterday's center rotation. What did you find the most challenging about the activity?

Student 1: I had a hard time coming up with an idea.

Student 2: Me too.

Ms. X. Ample: OK, remember when I gave you the writing starters list? That's a useful tool to get started.

Student 3: Yes, I used it, and I began my extended response with this claim. "Plastic island, the collection of plastics in the Pacific Ocean, directly affects the health of marine life."

Ms. X. Ample: Yes, you see how you made it a strong claim? It's a strong claim because you make a statement about the effects of plastics on marine life. How did you select your evidence?

Student 4: I had the same claim. I used the video that we saw about plastics asphyxiating turtles.

Ms. X. Ample: Great. That's a solid piece of evidence, but how does that affect the health of marine life?

Student 1: It affects the marine life because it's all connected. If the turtles die, it affects something else in the food chain.

The teacher and students continue to discuss the different pieces of evidence that they used to create a written evidence based argument, "Plastic island, the collection of plastics in the Pacific Ocean, directly affects the health of marine life."

There are a couple of important elements to emphasize in this brief excerpt. Notice that the teacher, Ms. X Ample, identifies what the students are mastering and identifies what they need to do to advance to greater development of literacy skills and content knowledge. Ms. X. Ample highlights when the student identifies a strong piece of evidence, for example, but also urges the student to develop the connection between the claim and evidence. The skill of marshaling evidence to support a claim is essential to this assignment, and through the Teacher-Led Center students can be compelled to put that skill into action.

Self- and Peer Assessment

Descriptive feedback doesn't have to come from the teacher. In peer assessment, students provide feedback to each other. In self-assessment, students assess themselves.

The greatest challenge most teachers find with peer assessment is creating an opportunity for students to give each other meaningful feedback, while also maintaining a safe classroom environment. In the LLC instructional model, students have multiple opportunities to provide feedback to each other in various centers. Giving students guidelines and rubrics in order to encourage them to focus on the learning goals is useful for this purpose. However, the single most valuable thing a teacher can do is to model appropriate feedback. When a class observes the teacher giving constructive, specific feedback that encourages student improvement, they're more likely to be able to do it themselves. Once students are comfortable with honest, nonjudgmental peer feedback, it will help immensely to promote learning. After all, one of the greatest benefits of peer assessment is that students really do learn from their classmates' successes and mistakes.

Self-assessment encourages students to think self-reflectively by examining their own work, based on the feedback they've given to others. When students think metacognitively about their learning in this way, they begin to accept responsibility for lifelong learning.

They learn to plan for their own education and to monitor their own progress. This is the ultimate goal of formative assessment and of education in general. It has been argued that assessment methods that leave out this valuable component are insufficient because they lose their effectiveness whenever the teacher (or other evaluator) is removed. As educational theorist D. Royce Sadler (1989) famously pointed out:

A key premise is that for students to be able to improve, they must develop the capacity to monitor the quality of their own work during actual production. This in turn requires that students possess an appreciation for what high quality work is, that they have the evaluative skill necessary for them to compare with some objectivity the quality of what they are producing in relation to the higher standard, and that they develop a store of tactics or moves which can be drawn upon to modify their own work. It is argued that these skills can be developed by providing direct, authentic evaluative experience for students. Instructional systems which do not make explicit provision for the acquisition of evaluative expertise are deficient, because they set up artificial but potentially removable performance ceilings for students (119).

Collaboration

Students who see themselves as partners in the learning process will commit to being involved in their own learning. This means that a culture of trust and open communication must exist. A truly collaborative classroom is founded on a sense of trust between all participants. When a respectful, trusting relationship is built between teacher and students, it will also improve students' ability to get along with each other. The classroom needs to be a place of mutual respect and appreciation so that each student can be secure and confident pursuing his or her goals.

In an ideal situation, the collaborative nature of education would extend beyond the classroom walls. Entire schools and school districts would support each student's individual learning process, encouraging self-assessment, peer assessment, and open communication between administrators, teachers, and learners.

These attributes of formative assessment underline that formative assessment is not one particular kind of measurement or tool. Rather, it is a multifaceted process that is integral and fundamental to the effective practice of teaching and learning.

Now, let's see an example of what formative assessment looks like as part of the Literacy & Learning Centers instructional model.

Case Study: Farmington, NM

Over a three-year period, with my assistance and the assistance of the Engaging Learners team, the Farmington, NM, Municipal Schools implemented skills-based grading for Grades K–8. For the purpose of this case study, we will first look at the district-wide instructional model. Then we'll focus on how teachers in two classrooms at Hermosa Middle School combined a skills-based grading system, built on the premises of formative assessment, within a Literacy & Learning Centers instructional model, with *Sadlier's Progress®, Vocabulary Workshop®, Grammar Workshop,* or *Grammar for Writing®*.

Farmington Municipal Schools Model of Instruction

Let's begin by considering the Farmington Model of Instruction, the district's unifying standard for describing and discussing effective teaching. Its primary goal is to improve teaching practices through a consistent observation and feedback process that translates to "student learning." This model was sharedwidely with teachers, administrators, and all district stakeholders.

The model of instruction identifies seven areas of effective pedagogy: feedback, new knowledge, deepen and practice, generate and test hypotheses, engagement, classroom management, and relationships. Each area of the model has a corresponding protocol. The protocols include a common rubric system that allows teachers to rate themselves, reflect, and collect evidence based upon set expectations for each area of pedagogy. Supervisors use the model and its protocols to make systematic observations and provide timely and meaningful feedback to their teachers.

The Farmington Model of Instruction sets expectations for effective teaching and learning for the entire district, but still empowers classroom teachers and their instructional decision-making. The protocols become a consistent, reliable measure across the district and provide principals an effective observation and evaluation tool.

Farmington Municipal Schools Proficiency Scales

Teachers in the same content area began by using the same proficiency scales, similar to the sample ELA proficiency scale on PAGE 71. So the expectations for all students were consistent throughout the school district.

Based on the Model of Instruction, the teachers and district leaders created grade- and course-specific proficiency scales to be used with their students. Each of these proficiency scales focused on the content topics and on the skills that the students needed to develop during each two- to three-week cycle.

Farmington's extensive, detailed proficiency scale document is divided into grade and content-area sections, with each section specifying its own simple and complex student goals for *each* topic in *each* quarter.

A sample **Proficiency Scale** from the Grade 8 English Language Arts is on PAGES 75 & 76. You can see the students' clearly defined simple and complex goals, but notice that the proficiency scales allow individual teachers to develop assignments and assessments, as they deem necessary.

  ENGAGING™ LEARNERS

Domain: The Art of Reading and Writing
Topic: Word Choice and Meaning

4.0 I know all of the Simple and Complex Learning Goals and my understanding goes beyond the grade level target.

COMPLEX
3.0 I know all of the Simple and Complex Learning Goals.
Academic Vocabulary: verbal irony   sarcasm

■ C1: Acquire and use accurately grade-appropriate general academic and domain-specific words and phrases describing argumentation and effective figure of speech usage. (L.8.11.6. 6)
  • Demonstrate understanding by using domain-specific words and phrases to identify argumentative elements in published and student-composed texts.
  • Demonstrate understanding by identifying and commenting on effective figures of speech in published and student-composed texts.
  • Demonstrate understanding by using effective figures of speech in written and spoken tasks.
■ C2: Determine or clarify the meaning of unknown and multiple-meaning words and phrases based on grade 8 reading and content, choosing flexibly from a range of strategies. (L.8.11.4.4)
  • Consult reference materials (e.g., dictionaries, glossaries, thesauruses), both print and digital, to research the etymology and historical uses of a word or phrase.
  • Compare different reference sources for differences in representation of word meaning, etymology and/or historical use.
■ C3: Demonstrate understanding of idioms, word relationships, and nuances in word meanings to extend word consciousness. (L.8.11.5.5)
  • Interpret figures of speech (verbal irony, sarcasm) in context.
  • Demonstrate applied understanding through selection and application of appropriate figures of speech on written tasks.
  • Demonstrate understanding through selection and application of appropriately nuanced word choices in written tasks.

2.5 I know all of the Simple Learning Goals and some of the Complex Learning Goals.

SIMPLE
2.0 I know all of the Simple Learning Goals.
Academic Vocabulary: claim evidence reasoning counterclaim qualifier rebuttal

■ S1: Review and use accurately grade-appropriate general academic and domain-specific words and phrases describing argumentation and effective word choice; gather vocabulary knowledge when considering a word or phrase important to comprehension or expression. (L.8.11.6.6)
  • Demonstrate understanding by using domain-specific words and phrases (claim, evidence, reasoning, counterclaim, qualifier, rebuttal) to identify argumentative elements in published and student-composed texts.
  • Demonstrate understanding by identifying and commenting on effective word choices in published and student-composed texts, and by suggesting alternatives to ineffective word choices.
■ S2: Determine or clarify the meaning of unknown and multiple-meaning words and phrases based on grade 7 reading and content, choosing flexibly from a range of strategies. (L.8.11.4.4)
  • Use context (e.g., the overall meaning of a sentence or paragraph; a word's position or function in a sentence) as a clue to the meaning of a word or phrase.
  • Use common, grade-appropriate Greek or Latin affixes and roots as clues to the meaning of a word (e.g., recede, precede, secede). Recognize when words suggest non-Greek or Latin language origins.
  • Consult general and specialized reference materials (e.g., dictionaries, glossaries, thesauruses), both print and digital, to find the pronunciation of a word or determine or clarify its precise meaning or its part of speech.
  • Verify the preliminary determination of the meaning of a word or phrase (e.g., by checking the inferred meaning in context or in a dictionary).
■ S3: Demonstrate understanding of figurative language, word relationships, and nuances in word meanings to extend word consciousness. (L.8.11.5.5 partial)
Interpret figures of speech (e.g. puns, onomatopoeia) in context.
  • Use the relationship between particular words to better understand each of the words.
  • Distinguish among the connotations (associations) of words with similar denotations (definitions) (e.g., *bullheaded, willful, firm, persistent, resolute*).

1.5 I know some of the Simple Learning Goals.

0.5 I know only one of the Simple Learning Goals.

0.0 I show no evidence of knowing the Learning Goals.

Domain: The Art of Reading and Writing
Topic: Word Choice and Meaning

SUCCESS CRITERIA

C1: Acquire and use accurately grade-appropriate general academic and domain-specific words and phrases describing argumentation and effective figure of speech usage.

- Students will be able to readily identify basic argumentative elements (claim, evidence, reasoning) in published and student-composed texts.

- Students will be able to readily identify phrases and words commonly used in qualifier and rebuttal statements within an argument.

- Students will be able to identify and comment on effective word choices demonstrating irony, sarcasm, in published and student-composed texts.

- Students will be able to use a variety of figures of speech in written and spoken tasks.

C2: Determine or clarify the meaning of unknown and multiple-meaning words and phrases based on grade 8 reading and content, choosing flexibly from a range of strategies.

- Students will be able to identify common, grade-appropriate affixes and roots as clues to the meaning of a word.

- Students will be able to identify times when words diverge from the Greek and Latin-derived root pattern.

- Students will be able to consult reference materials (e.g., dictionaries, glossaries, thesauruses), both print and digital, to research the etymology and historical uses of a word or phrase.

- Students will be able to compare different reference sources for differences in representation of word meaning, etymology and/or historical use.

C3: Demonstrate understanding of idioms, word relationships, and nuances in word meanings to extend word consciousness.

- Students will be able to interpret idiomatic phrases in context to demonstrate understanding of their literal meaning as well as some element of a phrase's historical origins.

- Students will be able to identify and comment on effective word choices demonstrating irony, sarcasm, and other figures of speech learned throughout middle school in published and student-composed texts.

- Students will be able to use a variety of figures of speech in 8th grade level written and spoken tasks.

In well-crafted proficiency scales, the clearly articulated simple and complex goals give teachers and students access to course-specific goals without restricting the way in which those goals are achieved. Notice that goals are not lesson plans. The "Success Criteria" provides a roadmap for one-on-one feedback at the Teacher-Led Center.

ENGAGING™ LEARNERS

Applying it in the Classroom

Now let's discuss how Shelly Johnson, a 6th grade teacher at the Hermosa Middle School, Farmington, NM, and her colleague, 8th grade teacher Adrienne Clerici, used the district-wide instructional model and the detailed, course-specific, proficiency scales to provide effective student evaluations during Teacher-Led Literacy & Learning Centers.

In Ms. Johnson and Ms. Clerici's classrooms, students shared their work in Teacher-Led Centers. The teachers used the proficiency scales as a tool to determine how students were developing their skills and as a reference for valuable descriptive feedback. In other words, the detailed proficiency scales identified learning goals, and the structure of the Literacy & Learning Center model provided the time for both one-on-one feedback and student self-reflection. Conversations in the Teacher-Led Center consisted of both the teacher and student comparing demonstrated skills to the skills they were expected to have. Students were encouraged to self-reflect and plan their next steps.

This skills-based grading system worked as a tool for formative assessment that benefited both teacher and student equally. Teachers found they could provide descriptive feedback in order to elaborate on vital parts of the lesson, and students were able to monitor their progress while still in the midst of completing an assignment. In the Farmington Municipal School classrooms, this type of assessment effectively informed students on how they were progressing toward the level of proficiency as articulated in both the simple and complex goals.

Some Final Thoughts

Immediate and descriptive feedback has been well documented to best meet the needs of students as they develop literacy skills and content knowledge (McManus 2008; Jensen 2009). Especially for teachers of older students, who commonly see over 100 or even 150 students per school day, keeping up with each student can seem an insurmountable challenge. I am often asked by colleagues, "How can I provide immediate and descriptive feedback when I teach so many students?" I won't dispute that it's a challenge. Yet, I often suggest that we think instead of providing feedback to groups of 4-5 students in a Teacher-Led Center. This provides ample opportunity to reinforce the students' strengths and provide suggestions for the development of vital skills and content knowledge. This has been key to the success of several school districts where I have implemented the Literacy & Learning Center model. Instead of thinking about providing feedback to your students every day, consider it over the course of a week. Ask yourself, "Did I interact with every student over a five-day period in a Teacher-Led Center?" Most colleagues that I encounter are overwhelmed by the idea at first. But after they try it, they quickly realize that not only is it doable, it's also far more effective than whatever they were doing previously.

For a final word, I want to again touch on traditional letter grades, as we discussed at this chapter's beginning. The research is quite clear that letter grades can have a profound effect on student progress. Letter grades and numerical grades become a statement that does little to indicate the growth and development of skills and content knowledge.

Chapter References and Resources

Cox, K. B. (2011). Putting classroom grading on the table: A reform in progress. *American Secondary Education*, 40(1), 67-87.

Dueck, M. (2014). *Grading smarter, not harder: Assessment strategies that motivate kids and help them learn.* Alexandria, VA: ASCD.

Dweck, C. S. (2006). *Mindset: The new psychology of success.* New York, NY: Random House.

Farmington Muncipal Schools. (2017). *FMS model of instruction and proficiency scales.* Retrieved from http://district.fms.k12.nm.us/Departments/Curriculum_and_Instruction/Curriculum

Heritage, M. (2010). *Formative assessment: Making it happen in the classroom.* Corwin Press.

Greenstein, L. (2010). *Chapter 1: The fundamentals of formative assessment. In L. Greenstein, What teachers really need to know about formative assessment.* Alexandria, VA: Association for Supervision & Curriculum Development.

Jensen, E. (2009). *Teaching with poverty in mind: What being poor does to kids' brains and what schools can do about it.* Alexandria, VA: Association for Supervision & Curriculum Development.

Marzano, R. (2000). *Transforming classroom grading.* Alexandria, VA: ASCD.

Marzano (2003) *What Works in Schools: Translating Research into Action.* Alexandria, VA: ASCD.

Marzano, R. J., & Heflebower, T. (2011). Grades that show what students know. *Educational Leadership*, 69(3), 34-39.

McKnight, K. S. (2016). Formative assessment strategies: An essential element for effective classrooms. In K.S. McKnight (Ed.), *Addressing the needs of all learners in the era of changing standards: Helping our most vulnerable students succeed through teaching flexibility, innovation, and creativity.* Lanham, MD: Rowman & Littlefield.

McManus, S. (2008). Paper prepared for the Formative Assessment for Teachers and Students State Collaborative on Assessment and Student Standards of the Council of Chief State School Officers. *Attributes of effective formative assessment.* Washington, DC: The Council of Chief State School Officers.

Moss, C. M., & Brookhart, S. M. (2019). *Advancing formative assessment in every classroom: A guide for instructional leaders.* ASCD.

Muñoz, M. A., & Guskey, T. R. (2015). *Standards-based grading and reporting will improve education.* Phi Delta Kappan, 96(7), 64-68.

O'Connor, K. (2009). *How to grade for learning, K-12 (3rd ed.).* Thousand Oaks, CA: Corwin.

Sadler, D. R. (1989). *Formative assessment and the design of instructional systems.* Instructional Science, 18(2), 119-144.

Scriffiny, P. L. (2008). Seven reasons for standards based grading. *Educational Leadership*, 66(2), 70-74.

Wormeli, R. (2018). *Fair isn't always equal: Assessing & grading in the differentiated classroom.* Stenhouse Publishers.

CHAPTER SIX
Teacher Tips and Additional Advice

CHAPTER SIX

Teacher Tips and Additional Advice

When I introduce Literacy & Learning Centers in schools, there are always questions about structure and implementation. In this final chapter, I hope to provide as much advice as I can and offer suggestions to make the transition to Literacy & Learning Centers as seamless as possible. I created a series of teacher tip videos that are on my YouTube channel, **https://bit.ly/2Mj6vNW**. I have included links and QR codes that you can easily scan to access these videos from your cell phone or tablet.

How many students should be in a group?

Generally, it is best to have no more than 4-5 students in a group. If you recall, earlier in the book we discussed that students should be grouped based on interest, readiness or ability. If there are more than five students in a group, they tend to branch off and form mini groups. I learned from working with colleagues in East St. Louis that when the students were getting off task, the simplest solution was to make the groups smaller. Yes, make the groups smaller. Put them into groups of three.

Ms. X Ample has 27 students in her sophomore world studies course. They are a chatty group of students who can be easily distracted. She decides to make smaller groups but does not want to increase the total number of centers. Therefore, she duplicated the centers and it looks like this:

Ms. Example Center Plan

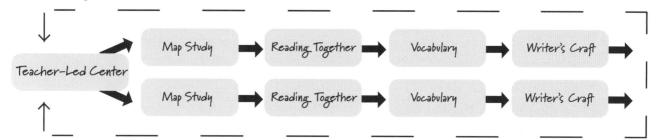

When the students rotate to the Teacher-Led Center, Ms. X Ample has the students from both Writer's Craft Centers join her. Although her Teacher-Led Center is larger with six students, they divide again into groups of three while working independently in the other centers. Here's some additional advice about group size from Hermosa Middle School Teachers, **https://youtu.be/YCZvUIoouSk**.

How long should each center be?

We know from neuroscience that attention spans are generally our chronological age times one. As a 53 year-old woman, my attention span should be 53 minutes. A high school freshman would be about 14 minutes (McClelland, Acock, Piccinin, Rhea & Stallings, 2013). Each Literacy & Learning Center should be between 10-18 minutes, depending on the age of the students.

How can I keep my students on task when they are working independently in centers?

There are several techniques that contribute to the development of student independence in centers.

Written Directions

When students are off task, it is usually in response to unclear instructions and procedures. To avoid this, I stress the importance of written directions. General directions and expectations for Literacy & Learning Centers should be posted in the classroom. Directions for each center activity should be written. For additional tips on written directions, see **https://youtu.be/pGzBYcTo488**.

Posted Classroom Norms

In addition to the written directions for each center, post the norms for Literacy & Learning Centers and classroom work. Avoid statements like, "Don't be distracted!" or "Don't take your group off task!" Not only are these vague statements that convey unclear expectations, these are punitive sounding statements. Instead, classroom norms should use generative language. For example, "Be sure to read all of the directions" or "Get input from all of your group members." When creating classroom norms, generative language promotes self-efficacy and tends to be more specific.

Timer

A classroom timer that is posted for the students to see while they work in centers supports them to work independently. It is amazing to me how important and influential a timer can be in keeping students on task. I was in a 9th grade science class last year and the teacher and I noticed that the students appeared to be off task and not using the allotted time wisely. I suggested that we use a timer and project it on the whiteboard at the front of the classroom. The effect was immediate. We noticed that students would look at the timer and remind their peers that they needed to stay focused. We no longer needed a signal to transition the students to the new centers. The students did it all on their own. When the students noticed that there were about 30 seconds left, they packed up the materials and moved to the next center. The students became more independent and more conscious of deadlines and time. For additional tips on using a timer during centers, see **https://youtu.be/FFqbZEcuack**.

Visual Directions and Center Map

Especially for younger students in grades 4 or 5, providing a visual map and explaining the center rotation is helpful. It can also be a useful tool for older students when you are first introducing Literacy & Learning Centers for your students. For additional tips on using a center map and visual directions during centers, see **https://youtu.be/Cf-IfDVaw8s**.

Redirection and Verbal Reminders

It is important to establish routines and procedures with students to increase focus and self-regulation, which contributes to greater student independence. When students are off task, stop the class, remind them of the norms, and then have them continue this work.

Here's an example from a 7th grade science classroom last year in which I was co-teaching.

> Students were working on an environmental unit, using Literacy & Learning Centers. After a few minutes the conversation got louder and they were clearly discussing topics other than their center activities. My co-teacher, Ms. Smith, and I redirected the students.
>
> **Dr. McKnight:** I need your attention in 5, 4, 3, 2, 1. Eyes on me. Now that I have your attention I want to remind you of center norm 3 which states, "If I can hear individual voices, it's too loud for academic work." I hear individual voices. Let's get back on task. Thank you.
>
> The students were back on task for about 5 minutes when the volume and off-task behavior again increased. Ms. Smith repeated the reminder.
>
> **Ms. Smith:** I need your attention in 5,4,3,2,1. Eyes on me. OK, so remember, center norm 3 states, "If I can hear individual voices, it's too loud for academic work." Let's get control of our voices and get back to work. Thank you.
>
> At first Ms. Smith and I had to remind the students of the classroom norms frequently. However, as the students continued to work in centers, our reminders became less frequent. After three months of consistent, generative and positive language the students rarely needed reminders. Their academic work improved and they worked with greater independence.

If we want students to develop independence in their academic work, we must model our expectations. Notice that the language in this example is always positive and redirects the students' attention to the established norms and expectations for work in Literacy & Learning Centers.

What suggestions do you have for organization of student work and materials?

There are many dimensions to Literacy & Learning Center organization. Every classroom is slightly different so most decisions that you will make will depend on your context. Here is some advice for organizing student work and materials.

Organizing Materials at Centers

Many teachers that I have worked with find it helpful to organize the materials that are needed for each center before the center rotations begin. Adrienne Clerici, an 8th grade teacher at Hermosa Middle School, uses baskets to store all the materials that are needed for each center. Remember, the goal of Literacy & Learning Centers is to increase student self-regulation and independence while practicing literacy skills and acquiring content knowledge. Organizing materials and written instructions eliminates distraction and contributes greatly to student success. See this video where Adrienne Clerici explains how to use baskets for center organization, **https://youtu.be/K_BtT2zVk9o**.

Organizing Completed Student Work

There are many ways that student work can be organized. Some teachers keep portfolios or folders of student work. Shelly Johnson, a 6th grade middle school teacher, organizes student work into folders. The students are responsible for maintaining their folders placing their work into the folders as it is completed. If your students have access to laptops, another strategy is to set up a portfolio system in Google Drive. In addition to Google Drive, your district might have a system already in place for student portfolios. These digital options are great because they cut down on paper, and they prepare students for the future since most colleges require students to submit work electronically. See how Shelley Johnson organizes student work in this video, **https://youtu.be/a-fCpqNF29o**.

How can I ensure that all students are working and participating at each center?

It is important that each student contributes to group and center work. One strategy to facilitate shared responsibility is to assign roles for each student. Marie Frost, a 6th grade teacher, uses student role sticks. Each center role is labeled on the stick. Of course the exact roles will vary depending on the nature of the center and the number of students in each group. Here are some sample roles:

Facilitator/Leader: Reads directions, passes out materials, makes sure all voices are heard and represented.

Timekeeper: Monitors time and keeps the group focused.

Recorder: Compiles group members' ideas in writing (i.e. graphic organizer).

Skeptic/Questioner: Addresses whether the group has considered all possibilities and points of view.

Initiator/Contributor: Contributes ideas and suggestions. Can propose new ideas and solutions.

Information Seeker: Asks for clarification and confirms information through fact checking.

Diagnostician: Identifies and indicates problems.

Prioritizer: Decides the order in which tasks/problems should be addressed.

Energizer: Raises or maintains the group's level of enthusiasm.

Using role sticks ensures that there is random selection or tasks and the students vary their roles.

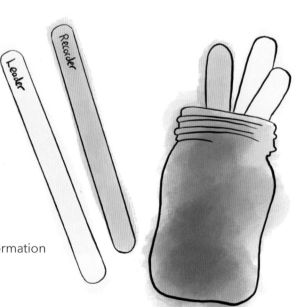

How can I increase student independence?

Most of academic standards promote student independence in applying skills. A strategy that I learned from a teacher in Murfeesboro, TN is a cup monitoring system.

Just like a raised hand, colored cups can be seen from anywhere in the room. But cups communicate more than a raised hand! They allow students to proceed with their work until the teacher is able to address their concerns.

Explain that during centers, the teacher needs to be free to travel the classroom to check on different groups and/or participate in a Teacher-Led Center.

Use a stack of plastic drinking cups at each center, and encourage students to put the appropriate colored cup on top.

Green - Full speed ahead. Everything is good. Students understand the task and are proceeding.
Yellow - Proceeding with caution. Students can start/continue with the task but have questions or problems.
Red - Stopped. Students are unable to work on the task.
Blue - Task is completed.

Try to be consistent about the colors and their meanings. I've even found that it's helpful to have all the teachers in a school use the same color system. That means students won't have to learn different color systems for different classes. But of course if you can't find the right color cups, it's okay to swap out something else! The actual color of the cups doesn't matter as long as your students understand your code. See an example of a Cups Monitoring System poster in Appendix B.

When students have a reliable method for requesting assistance, it drastically decreases distractions. Students learn to monitor their own work and independence increases. As teachers, if we move from center to center and ask, "Do you have any questions," it can take students five times longer to get back on task and refocus. We never want to interrupt students while they are working unless it is necessary. In this video, Shelley Johnson explains how she uses the cup monitoring system in her classroom, **https://youtu.be/2tePq52ZZ5E**.

What happens when a student finishes early or does not have enough time to complete a center activity?

No matter how hard I try, I am not able to perfectly time my centers. That's why I always include a make-up or reflection center. At this center, students have the opportunity to complete any unfinished work and reflect on their center work. I encourage students to identify their best work and the work that was most challenging. In the next center rotation, I can consult with the students' self-assessment of their work. Many teachers create a list of reminders and suggestions for the make-up/reflection center. Adrienne Clerici is masterful with her implementation of the make-up/reflection center for her students. Learn how she sets up this center, **https://youtu.be/blKwT7b-P4**.

Some Final Thoughts

The Literacy & Learning Center model is based on my work and experiences in numerous classrooms and it is built on research that indicates the best practices for the development of literacy skills. Remember that although this book is filled with suggestions and resources, the Literacy & Learning Center model is malleable. Make whatever adjustments are necessary to meet the needs of your students.

Chapter References and Resources

Barkley, E.F., Cross, K.P., & Major, C.H. (2005). *Collaborative learning techniques*. San Francisco: Jossey-Bass.

McClelland, M. M., Acock, A. C., Piccinin, A., Rhea, S. A., & Stallings, M. C. (2013). Relations between preschool attention span-persistence and age 25 educational outcomes. *Early Childhood Research Quarterly*, 28(2), 314-324.

ENGAGING™ LEARNERS

APPENDIX A

Selecting and Grouping Texts

APPENDIX A

Selecting and Grouping Texts
Revising a Unit – Build It Around an Essential Question

A 7th grade ELA teaching team had a unit based around the book, Of Mice and Men by John Steinbeck. Every year they taught the same book. As the teachers, curriculum director and I evaluated the effectiveness of the unit we determined that:

- The majority of students were able to read the text independently or with minimal support.

- A few students struggled with the text, even with teacher support.

- Many students were totally uninterested in the book and didn't really finish it.

- Classroom activities centered around "proving that you read the assigned pages".

- Lessons focused on remembering and understanding (the lowest levels of Bloom's Taxonomy) and rarely approached analyzing, applying, evaluating, or creating.

The teaching team wanted to rework the unit to incorporate differentiated instruction and hopefully inspire all of the students to more actively engage with the text.

One of the easiest ways to incorporate differentiated instruction into the classroom is to build units around essential questions instead of a specific text. It isn't difficult, has measurable advantages, and once the planning is done, the same unit can be used over and over. So it's worth the investment!

ENGAGING™
LEARNERS

What is an Essential Question?

Essential questions are big questions that require a student to explore a topic and reflect on the meaning of texts. They are never yes/no questions; in fact, essential questions often don't have one right answer. For more information about essential questions and how to use them, read Understanding by Design by Grant Wiggins and Jay McTigue.

At first, the idea of letting students choose novels - and knowing that your class is reading several novels at the same time - can be intimidating. Remember, the focus is on the skills and the novel is the vehicle to develop key literacy skills. In the Literacy & Learning Center model, the students work in centers with clearly stated focus. For example, in the Vocabulary Center, the students work on an activity and using their chosen novel to study words and language. In the Reading Together Center, the students are practicing an annotated note taking strategy with their chosen book.

The book lists on the following pages offer a selection of fictional and non-fictional texts that are centered around an essential question, and are ideal for the Literacy & Learning Center model. Notice that the texts include a range of complexity levels to help differentiate and include all learners. Use these examples as inspiration as you create your own book lists.

Fourth Grade

Topic: Journeys Non-Fiction

Essential Question: How does discovering new lands expand our knowledge?

TEXT COMPLEXITY	BOOK TITLE	AUTHOR
4th-7th grade	A Journey to the New World, Mayflower 1620	Kathryn Lasky
2nd-5th grade	Hannah's Journey: The Story of an Immigrant Girl	Marissa Moss
2nd-5th grade	I Survived the Sinking of the Titanic, 1912	Lauren Tarshis
3rd-5th grade	If Your Name Was Changed at Ellis Island	Ellen Levine
3rd-5th grade	Surviving the Journey: The Story of the Oregon Trail	Danny Kravitz
3rd-4th grade	The Buffalo Soldiers and the American West	Jason Glasser
2nd-4th grade	Where Do You Think You're Going, Christoper Columbus?	Jean Fritz
3rd-7th grade	Who Was Amelia Earhart?	Kate Boehm Jerome
3rd-7th grade	Who Was Neil Armstrong?	Roberta Edwards

Fourth Grade

Topic: Journeys Fiction

Essential Question: What can we learn about ourselves when we leave home?

TEXT COMPLEXITY	BOOK TITLE	AUTHOR
K-4th grade	Apples to Oregon	Deborah Hopkinson
4th-8th grade	Bewitched in Oz	Laura J. Burns
3rd-7th grade	Dear Mr. Henshaw	Beverly Cleary
3rd-7th grade	Drita, My Homegirl	Jenny Lombard
3rd-7th grade	Elijah of Buxton	Christopher Paul Curtis
4th-7th grade	Eliza's Freedom Road: An Underground Railroad Diary	Jerdine Nolan
3rd-4th grade	Emma's New Beginning	Jessica Gunderson
3rd-6th grade	Gulliver's Travels	John Lemke
3rd-6th grade	In the Year of the Boar and Jackie Robinson	Bette Bao Lord
3rd-6th grade	Little House on Rocky Ridge	Roger Lea MacBride
3rd-6th grade	Sarah, Plain and Tall	Patricia MacLachlan
4th-7th grade	The Drum of Destiny	Christopher Stevenson
3rd-5th grade	The Last Rider: The Final Days of the Pony Express	J. Gunderson
4th-6th grade	The One and Only Ivan	Katherine Applegate
3rd-7th grade	The Wanderer	Sharon Creech
2nd-4th grade	Time Voyage (Return to Titanic)	Steve Brezenoff
2nd-4th grade	When Jessie Came Across the Sea	Amy Hest

Fourth Grade

Topic: Earth's Shifting Surfaces

Essential Question: How can humans prepare for the unpredictability of nature?

TEXT COMPLEXITY	BOOK TITLE	AUTHOR
2nd-5th grade	Earthquakes and Other Natural Disasters	Harriet Griffey
3rd-5th grade	Earth's Changing Crust	Rebecca Harman
3rd-4th grade	Endangered Energy: Investigating the Scarcity of Fossil Fuels	Rani Iyer
3rd-4th grade	Endangered Rain Forests: Investigating Rain Forests in Crisis	Rani Iyer
3rd-4th grade	Endangered Rivers: Investigating Rivers in Crisis	Rani Iyer
2nd-4th grade	Erosion	Becky Olien
K-4th grade	Erosion: Changing Earth's Surface	Robin Koontz
1st-8th grade	National Parks	Erin McHugh
3rd-4th grade	When Volcanoes Erupt	Nel Yomtov

Fourth Grade

Topic: Changes

Essential Question: What motivates people to try and change the world?

TEXT COMPLEXITY	BOOK TITLE	AUTHOR
2nd-5th grade	28 Days: Moments in Black History That Changed the World	Charles R. Smith, Jr. and Shane W. Evans
3rd-4th grade	Jake Burton Carpenter and the Snowboard	Micheal O'Hearn
K-4th grade	National Geographic Readers: Caterpillar to Butterfly	Laura F. Marsh
4th-6th grade	Renewable Energy: Discover the Fuel of the Future with 20 Projects	Joshua Sneideman and Erin Twamley
3rd-4th grade	Rosa Parks and the Montgomery Bus Boycott	Connie Colwell Miller
5th-8th grade	The Constitution and the Bill of Rights	Roben Alarcon
3rd-5th grade	The U.S. Constitution, Bill of Rights, and a New Nation	Steven Otfinoski
3rd-7th grade	They Stood Alone!: 25 Men and Women Who Made a Difference	Sandra McLeod Humphrey
3rd-7th grade	Who Was Eleanor Roosevelt?	Gare Thompson

Fourth Grade

Topic: Brave Adventures Fiction

Essential Question: What sets a hero apart from other people?

TEXT COMPLEXITY	BOOK TITLE	AUTHOR
2nd-4th grade	A Crazy Day with Cobras	Mary Pope Osbourne
1st-4th grade	Amber Was Brave, Essie Was Smart	Vera B. Williams
K-3rd grade	Brave Girl: Clara and the Shirtwaist Makers' Strike of 1909	Michelle Markel
1st-4th grade	Buzz Beaker and the Growing Goo	Cari Meister
3rd-7th grade	Charlie and the Chocolate Factory	Roald Dahl
3rd-7th grade	Danny, the Champion of the World	Roald Dahl
3rd-6th grade	Frindle	Andrew Clements
4th-8th grade	Guys Read: Other Worlds	Jon Scieszka
2nd-4th grade	Jake Drake, Bully Buster	Andrew Celements
4th-7th grade	Number the Stars	Lois Lowry
3rd-7th grade	Sailing to Freedom	Martha Bennett Stiles
3rd-7th grade	Sideways Stories from Wayside School	Louis Sachar
4th-7th grade	Survival Stories of the Almost Brave	Jen White
3rd-7th grade	Tales of a Fourth Grade Nothing	Judy Blume
3rd-7th grade	The Janitor's Boy	Andrew Clements
4th-9th grade	The Red Pyramid	Rick Riordan

Fourth Grade

Topic: Brave Adventures Non-Fiction

Essential Question: What is a courageous act?

TEXT COMPLEXITY	BOOK TITLE	AUTHOR
2nd-5th grade	A Time to Be Brave	Joan Betty Stuchner
3rd-7th grade	A Voice of Her Own: The Story of Phillis Wheatley, Slave	Kathryn Lasky
2nd-4th grade	Clara Barton: Angel of the Battlefield	TIME Magazine
2nd-5th grade	Dolley Madison: First Lady of the United States	Melissa Carosella
3rd-6th grade	George vs. George: The American Revolution as Seen from Both Sides	Rosalyn Schanzer
3rd-4th grade	George Washington: Leading a New Nation	Matt Doeden
1st-5th grade	Irena Sendler and the Children of the Warsaw Ghetto	Susan Goldman Rubin
2nd-5th grade	Climbing Everest	Gail Herman
1st-4th grade	Nobody Owns the Sky: The Story of "Brave Bessie" Coleman	Reeve Lindbergh
3rd-5th grade	Who Was Annie Oakley?	Stephanie Spinner

ENGAGING™
LEARNERS

Fourth Grade

Topic: Problem Solving Social Studies & Science

Essential Question: How can someone become a better scientific observer?

TEXT COMPLEXITY	BOOK TITLE	AUTHOR
2nd-4th grade	A More Perfect Union	Betsy Maestro
4th-7th grade	Let's Think About Sustainable Energy	Vic Parker
3rd-7th grade	A Kid's Guide to America's Bill of Rights	Kathleen Krull
4th-8th grade	The Quest for the Tree Kangaroo: An Expedition to the Cloud Forest of New Guinea	Sy Montgomery
4th-6th grade	The Story of Fossil Fuels	William B. Rice
1st-4th grade	Understanding the Bill of Rights	Sally Senzell Isaacs

Fourth Grade

Topic: Challenges in Traditional Literature

Essential Question: Why is it important to know where things came from?

TEXT COMPLEXITY	BOOK TITLE	AUTHOR
2nd-5th grade	Aesop's Fables	Ann McGovern
3rd-7th grade	The Chocolate Touch	Patrick Skene Catling
4th-6th grade	Jason and the Golden Fleece	Nel Yomtov
K-5th grade	John Henry	Julius Lester
4th-7th grade	Not One Damsel in Distress	Jane Yolen
4th-6th grade	Perseus and Medusa	Blake Hoena
4th-7th grade	Robin Hood	Aaron Shepard
4th-7th grade	Sir Gawain and the Green Knight	Michael Morpurgo
3rd-7th grade	Tales from the Odyssey, Part 1	Mary Pope Osborne
3rd-7th grade	The BFG	Roald Dahl
2nd-5th grade	The Dragon Prince	Laurance Yep
2nd-4th grade	The Elephant's Friend and Other Tales from Ancient India	Marcia Williams
K-4th grade	The Little Red Ant and the Great Big Crumb	Shirley Climo
2nd-4th grade	The Seven Voyages of Sinbad	Martin Powell
K-4th grade	The Tall Tale of Paul Bunyan	Martin Powell
K-4th grade	The Weaving of a Dream	Marilee Powell
K-4th grade	Theseus and the Minotaur	Nel Yomtov
K-4th grade	When the Sun and the Moon Live in the Sky	Elphinstone Dayrell

Fourth Grade

Topic: Science

Essential Question: What makes people curious about the world?

TEXT COMPLEXITY	BOOK TITLE	AUTHOR
4th-7th grade	21st Century: Mysteries of Deep Space	Stephanie Paris
4th-7th grade	22nd Century: Future of Space	Stephanie Kuligowski
3rd-6th grade	Aliens and UFOs	Lori Hile
4th-8th grade	Battling Extinction	Tamra B. Orr
K-5th grade	Bones	Seymour Simon
4th-5th grade	Destined for Space: Our Story of Exploration	Don Nardo
3rd-5th grade	Eyes and Ears	Seymour Simon
K-4th grade	Feel the Wind	Arthur Dorros
4th-7th grade	Forensic Science Investigator	Tamra B. Orr
3rd-6th grade	Mysteries of Alien Visitors and Abductions	Kathryn Walker
3rd-5th grade	Nuclear Energy	Chris Oxlade
3rd-6th grade	Our Solar System	Seymour Simon
4th-7th grade	The Polar Bear Scientists	Peter Lourie
4th-8th grade	Restoring Structures	Jennifer Zeiger
3rd-4th grade	Take Off! All About Airplanes	Jennifer Prior
4th-8th grade	The Park Scientists: Gila Monsters, Geysers and Grizzly Bears	Mary Kay Carson
2nd-4th grade	The Secrets of Earth	Emma Carlson-Berne
3rd-4th grade	The Worst Earthquakes of All Time	Mary Englar
2nd-5th grade	Tsunamis and Other Natural Disasters	Mary Pope Osborne

Fourth Grade

Topic: Amazing Discoveries

Essential Question: Why don't great inventors give up?

TEXT COMPLEXITY	BOOK TITLE	AUTHOR
3rd-4th grade	Alexander Graham Bell and the Telephone	Jennifer Fandel
3rd-4th grade	Bejamin Franklin: An American Genius	Kay Melchisedich Oslon
4th-7th grade	Earth and Space Science: The Wonder of Our Solar System	Lisa Greathouse
3rd-4th grade	Johann Gutenberg and the Printing Press	Kay Melchisedich Oslon
3rd-4th grade	Levi Strauss and Blue Jeans	National Geographic
4th-7th grade	Out of the Darkness: The Story of Louis Braille	Russel Freedman
3rd-4th grade	The Television	Richard Spilsbury
3rd-7th grade	What Color is My World?	Kareem Abdul Jabbar et al.
2nd-4th grade	What's the Big Idea, Ben Franklin?	Jean Fritz

Fifth Grade

Topic: Challenge Fiction

Essential Question: Why is it important to leave your comfort zone?

TEXT COMPLEXITY	BOOK TITLE	AUTHOR
4th-7th grade	Any Small Goodness: A Novel of the Barrio	Tony Johnston
4th-7th grade	Dangerous Waters: An Adventure on the Titanic	Gregory Mone
5th-8th grade	Elephant Run	Roland Smith
4th-8th grade	Found	Margaret Peterson Haddix
4th-6th grade	Ida B: . . . and Her Plans to Maximize Fun, Avoid Disaster, and (Possibly) Save the World	Katherine Kannigan
4th-7th grade	Joey Pigza Swallowed the Key	Jack Gantos
4th-5th grade	Jump Serve	Jake Maddox
3rd-7th grade	Lacrosse Firestorm	Matt Christopher
3rd-5th grade	The Lemonade War	Jacqueline Davies
3rd-5th grade	My Name is Maria Isabel	Alma Flor Ada
3rd-6th grade	No Talking	Andrew Clements
3rd-7th grade	On This Long Journey, the Journal of Jesse Smoke, A Cherokee Boy	Joseph Bruchac
4th-6th grade	Out of My Mind	Sharon M. Draper
3rd-7th grade	Out of the Dust	Karen Hesse
5th-8th grade	Rivals	Tim Green
2nd-5th grade	Roughing It on the Oregon Trail	Diane Stanley
4th-7th grade	Shakespeare's Secret	Elise Broach
5th-7th grade	Silhouetted by the Blue	Traci L. Jones
3rd-6th grade	Stone Fox	John Reynolds Gardiner
5th-8th grade	The Fellowship for Alien Detection	Kevin Emerson
2nd-5th grade	The Mighty Miss Malone	Christopher Paul Curtis
3rd-7th grade	The Troubles of Johnny Cannon	Isaiah Campbell
2nd-6th grade	The Year of the Panda	Miriam Schlein
4th-7th grade	You Can't Have My Planet: But Take My Brother, Please	James Mihaley

Fifth Grade

Topic: New Experiences Non-Fiction

Essential Question: How can we prepare for the unexpected?

TEXT COMPLEXITY	BOOK TITLE	AUTHOR
3rd-5th grade	George Eastman and the Kodak Camera	Jennifer Fandel
4th-7th grade	Iditarod Dream: Dusty and His Sled Dogs Compete in Alaska's Jr. Iditarod	Ted Wood
4th-7th grade	Orphan Train Rider: One Boy's True Story	Andrea Warren
4th-7th grade	Roller Coasters: From Concept to Consumer	Kevin Cunningham
3rd-5th grade	Skateboarding: How It Works	Emily Sohn

Fifth Grade

Topic: Laws of Motion

Essential Question: What kinds of forces affect the motion of objects?

TEXT COMPLEXITY	BOOK TITLE	AUTHOR
2nd-5th grade	Climbing and Diving: Forces of Motion	Lisa Greathouse
1st-5th grade	Experiments in Forces and Motion with Toys and Everyday Stuff	Emily Sohn
4th-7th grade	Forces and Motion: Investigating a Car Crash	Ian Graham
2nd-5th grade	Isaac Newton	Kay Barnham
3rd-5th grade	Isaac Newton and the Laws of Motion	Andra Gianopoulos
3rd-5th grade	Super Cool Forces and Motion Activities with Max Axiom	Agnieszka Biskup
5th-8th grade	The Gripping Truth about Forces and Motion	Agnieszka Biskup
3rd-5th grade	The Science of Baseball with Max Axiom, Super Scientist	David L. Dreier
3rd-5th grade	Thud!: Wile E. Coyote Experiments with Forces and Motion	Mark Weakland
3rd-5th grade	Vroom! Speed and Acceleration	Stephanie Paris

ENGAGING™ LEARNERS

Fifth Grade

Topic: Scientific Discoveries and Historical Lives

Essential Question: How are our lives different because of long ago discoveries?

TEXT COMPLEXITY	BOOK TITLE	AUTHOR
4th-8th grade	A Medal for Leroy	Michael Morpurgo
3rd-7th grade	Big Bad Ironclad!	Nathan Hale
4th-8th grade	Black Pioneers of Science and Invention	Louis Haber
4th-8th grade	Children of the Great Depression	Russell Freedman
5th-8th grade	Echo	Pam Munoz Ryan
3rd-7th grade	Electrical Wizard: How Nikola Tesla Lit Up the World	Elizabeth Rusch
5th-9th grade	Fever 1793	Laurie Halse Anderson
K-5th grade	Fly High: The Story of Bessie Coleman	Louise Borden
2nd-5th grade	If You Lived 100 Years Ago	Ann McGovern
2nd-5th grade	If You Lived in Colonial Times	Ann McGovern
4th-7th grade	Laura Ingalls Wilder: A Biography	William Anderson
3rd-6th grade	Mystery at Manzanar: A WWII Internment Camp Story	Eric Fein
3rd-7th grade	One Dead Spy	Nathan Hale
4th-7th grade	Out of the Darkness: The Story of Louis Braille	Russell Freedman
1st-5th grade	I Survived the Battle of Gettysburg, 1863	Lauren Tarshis
5th-9th grade	The Ransom of Mercy Carter	Caroline B. Cooney
5th-9th grade	The Voice That Challenged a Nation: Marian Anderson and the Struggle for Equal Rights	Russell Freedman
3rd-5th grade	Who Was Albert Einstein?	Jess Brallier

Fifth Grade

Topic: Risk Fiction

Essential Question: What are the right kinds of risks to take?

TEXT COMPLEXITY	BOOK TITLE	AUTHOR
4th-6th grade	Aliens Ate My Homework	Bruce Coville
3rd-7th grade	Aliens on Vacation	Clete Barrett Smith
4th-7th grade	Doll Bones	Holly Black
4th-7th grade	Extra Credit	Andrew Clements
4th-6th grade	Flora and Ulysses	Kate DiCamillo
3rd-7th grade	Frightful's Mountain	Jean Craighead George
4th-7th grade	Lawn Boy	Gary Paulsen
4th-7th grade	One Crazy Summer	Rita Williams-Garcia
3rd-7th grade	Ruby Holler	Sharon Creech
5th-9th grade	Semper Fido	C. Alexander London
5th-8th grade	Summer at Forsaken Lake	Michael D. Beil
3rd-5th grade	The Tale of Despereaux	Kate DiCamillo
3rd-7th grade	Walls Within Walls	Maureen Sherry

Fifth Grade

Topic: Risks and Perseverance Non-Fiction

Essential Question: What do we learn when taking a risk fails?

TEXT COMPLEXITY	BOOK TITLE	AUTHOR
5th-7th grade	Against All Odds	Glenn Stout
4th-8th grade	The California Gold Rush	Peter Benoit
5th-8th grade	Daring Play: How a Courageous Jackie Robinson Transformed Baseball	Michael Burgan
3rd-6th grade	Interrupted Journey: Saving Endangered Sea Turtles	Kathryn Lasky
3rd-5th grade	John Sutter and the California Gold Rush	Matt Doeden
1st-5th grade	The Wright Brothers: Inventors Whose Ideas Really Took Flight	Mike Venezia
3rd-7th grade	The Wright Brothers: Pioneers of American Aviation	Quentin Reynolds
3rd-5th grade	The Z-Boys and Skateboarding	Jameson Anderson
4th-8th grade	We Rode the Orphan Trains	Andrea Warren
3rd-7th grade	What Was The Lewis and Clark Expedition?	Judith St. George

ENGAGING™
LEARNERS

Fifth Grade

Topic: Ecosystems Non-Fiction

Essential Question: How are ecosystems affected by the actions of human beings?

TEXT COMPLEXITY	BOOK TITLE	AUTHOR
4th-8th grade	Climate Change: Discover How It Impacts Spaceship Earth	Joshua Sneideman
1st-5th grade	Deserts	Gail Glbbons
3rd-5th grade	Endangered Oceans: Investigating Oceans in Crisis	Jody S. Rake
3rd-5th grade	Exploring Ecosystems with Max Axiom, Super Scientist	Agnieszka Biskup
4th-8th grade	Climate Change: Discover How It Impacts Spaceship Earth	Joshua Sneideman
1st-5th grade	Deserts	Gail Glbbons
3rd-5th grade	Endangered Oceans: Investigating Oceans in Crisis	Jody S. Rake
3rd-5th grade	Exploring Ecosystems with Max Axiom, Super Scientist	Agnieszka Biskup
4th-7th grade	Extreme Animals: The Toughest Creatures on Earth	Nicola Davies
4th-8th grade	Inside Ecosystems and Biomes: Life Science	Debra J. Housel
5th-7th grade	Life and Non-Life in an Ecosystem	William B. Rice
4th-7th grade	The Ocean Biome	National Geographic Learning
4th-8th grade	Project Seahorse	Pamela S. Turner
1st-5th grade	Seymour Simon's Extreme Earth Records	Seymour Simon
1st-5th grade	The Great Kapok Tree: A Tale of the Amazon Rain Forest	Lynne Cherry
3r-7th grade	The Plant Hunters	Anita SIlvey
2nd-5th grade	What If There Were No Lemmings?	Suzanne Slade
5th-9th grade	World Without FIsh	Mark Kurlansky

Fifth Grade

Topic: Environmental Issues Non-Fiction

Essential Question: What are the consequences of changes to the environment?

TEXT COMPLEXITY	BOOK TITLE	AUTHOR
4th-6th grade	Are Humans Damaging the Atmosphere?	Catherine Chambers
2nd-6th grade	Ask an Expert: Climate Change	Richard Spilsbury
3rd-7th grade	Climate Change	DK Publishing
4th-6th grade	Coping With Population Growth	Nicola Barber
4th-7th grade	Plastic Pollution	Geof Knight
2nd-6th grade	Reducing Pollution and Waste	Jen Green
3rd-6th grade	Superstorm Sandy	Lynn Peppas
2nd-6th grade	Sustaining our Natural Resources	Jen Green
2nd-5th grade	What Can We Do about Acid Rain?	David J. Jakubiak

Fifth Grade

Topic: General Mythology

Essential Question: How do characters in mythology relate to nature?

TEXT COMPLEXITY	BOOK TITLE	AUTHOR
4th-7th grade	Ali Baba: Fooling the Forty Thieves: An Arabian Tale	Marie Croall
4th-7th grade	Amateratsu: Return of the Sun	National Geographic Learning
3rd-7th grade	Beowulf: Monster Slayer: A British Legend	Paul D. Storrie
5th-8th grade	Chinese Myths and Legends	Anita Ganeri
4th-8th grade	Isis and Osiris: To the Ends of the Earth	Jeff Limke
3rd-6th grade	The Hero Twins: Against the Lords of Death	Dan Jolley
3rd-6th grade	The Lion, the Witch and the Wardrobe	C.S. Lewis
4th-7th grade	The Smoking Mountain: The Story of Popocatépetl and Iztaccíhuatl	Dan Jolley
4th-6th grade	Thor & Loki: In the Land of Giants	Jeff Limke
4th-7th grade	Yu the Great: Conquering the Flood: A Chinese Legend	Paul D. Storrie

Fifth Grade

Topic: General Mythology

Essential Question: How are gods and heroes alike and different in Greek myths?

TEXT COMPLEXITY	BOOK TITLE	AUTHOR
3rd-7th grade	Amazing Greek Myths of Wonder and Blunders	Michael Townsend
4th-9th grade	Aphrodite: Goddess of Love	George O'Connor
4th-9th grade	Apollo: The Brilliant One	George O'Connor
4th-9th grade	Ares: Bringer of War	George O'Connor
4th-7th grade	Atalanta: The Race Against Destiny	Justine Fontes
4th-9th grade	Athena: Grey-Eyed Goddess	George O'Connor
4th-8th grade	Get Lost, Odysseus!	Kate McMullan
4th-9th grade	Hades: Lord of the Dead	George O'Connor
5th-9th grade	Hera: The Goddess and Her Glory	George O'Connor
3rd-7th grade	Percy Jackson's Greek Gods	Rick Riordan
4th-8th grade	Phone Home, Persephone!	Kate McMullan
5th-9th grade	Poseidon: Earth Shaker	George O'Connor
3rd-5th grade	Theseus and the Minotaur	Nel Yomtov
5th-9th grade	Zeus: King of the Gods	George O'Connor

Fifth Grade

Topic: Immigration

Essential Question: How do traditions change and stay the same when people move?

TEXT COMPLEXITY	BOOK TITLE	AUTHOR
5th-8th grade	A House of Tailors	Patricia Reilly Giff
4th-8th grade	Angel Island Immigration	Jamie Kallio
5th-8th grade	Bread and Roses, Too	Katherine Paterson
5th-10th grade	Flesh and Blood So Cheap: The Triangle Fire and Its Legacy	Albert Marrin
2nd-5th grade	If Your Name Was Changed at Ellis Island	Ellen Levine
4th-7th grade	Letters from Rifka	Karen Hesse
4th-8th grade	Lyddie	Katherine Paterson
3rd-7th grade	Maggie's Door	Patricia Reilly Giff
3rd-6th grade	Migration from Africa	Kevin Cunningham
6th-8th grade	Something About America	Maria Testa
5th-9th grade	The Brooklyn Nine	Alan M. Gratz
2nd-5th grade	The Lotus Seed	Sherry Garland
3rd-6th grade	The Sign of the Beaver	Elizabeth George Speare
4th-7th grade	Walk the Wild Road	Nigel Hinton

Sixth Grade

Topic: World Cultures Fiction

Essential Question: What qualities make someone a hero?

TEXT COMPLEXITY	BOOK TITLE	AUTHOR
6th-9th grade	The Odyssey	Gareth Hinds
2nd-6th grade	The Magic Pomegranate: A Jewish Folktale	Peninnah Schram
5th-7th grade	Adventures of the Greek Heroes	Anne Wiseman and Mollie McLean
4th-8th grade	The Adventures of Hercules	Martin Powell
5th-8th grade	African Myths and Legends	Catherine Chambers
5th-8th grade	Ancient Maya	Barbara A. Somervill
6th-9th grade	Beowulf: The Graphic Novel	Gareth Hinds
2nd-6th grade	Bokuden and the Bully: A Japanese Folktale	Stephen Krensky
5th-8th grade	Egyptian Myths and Legends	Fiona Macdonald
2nd-6th grade	Greek Myths	Deborah Lock
3rd-7th grade	Hard as Nails in Myths and Legends	Tracey Turner
5th-8th grade	Norse Myths and Legends	Anita Ganeri
1st-6th grade	The Earth Under Sky Bear's Feet: Native American Poems of the Land	Joseph Bruchac
2nd-6th grade	The Gods and Goddesses of Olympus	Aliki

Sixth Grade

Topic: Non-Fiction Narratives

Essential Question: What do we have in common with those who lived in the past?

TEXT COMPLEXITY	BOOK TITLE	AUTHOR
6th-12th grade	Hidden Like Anne Frank: 14 True Stories of Survival	Marcel Prins
5th-8th grade	Surviving Hitler: A Boy in the Nazi Death Camps	Andrea Warren
5th-9th grade	Remember Pearl Harbor: American and Japanese Survivors Tell Their Stories	Thomas B. Allen
3rd-6th grade	Smooth Sea and a Fighting Chance: The Story of the Sinking of Titanic	Steven Otfinoski
6th-9th grade	Soul Surfer: A True Story of Faith, Family and Fighting to Get Back on the Board	Bethany Hamilton
3rd-6th grade	The Apache Indians	Bill Lund
3rd-6th grade	The Sioux Indians	Bill Lund
4th-7th grade	Always Inventing: A Photobiography of Alexander Graham Bell	Tom L. Matthews

Sixth Grade

Topic: Exploration Non-Fiction

Essential Question: How have new discoveries changed the way we live?

TEXT COMPLEXITY	BOOK TITLE	AUTHOR
3rd-6th grade	Ancient Egypt: Beyond the Pyramids	Kathleen W. Deady
5th-8th grade	Lewis and Clark: Opening the American West	Ellen Rodger
2nd-6th grade	Leif Eriksson	Shannon Knudsen
6th-12th grade	No Summit out of Sight: The True Story of the Youngest Person to Climb the Seven Summits	Jordan Romero
6th-10th grade	Out of Bounds: Seven Stories of Conflict and Hope	Beverley Naidoo
5th-8th grade	Robert Peary vs. Frederick Cook: Race to the North Pole	Ellis Roxburgh
3rd-6th grade	Sylvia Earle: Ocean Explorer	Dennis Fertig
3rd-7th grade	Who Was Jacques Cousteau?	Nico Medina
3rd-7th grade	Who Was King Tut?	Roberta Edwards

Sixth Grade

Topic: Historical Fiction

Essential Question: How have people changed since the eras in these works?

TEXT COMPLEXITY	BOOK TITLE	AUTHOR
6th-10th grade	All My Noble Dreams and Then What Happens	Gloria Whelan
5th-8th grade	The Aztec News	Philip Steele
3rd-7th grade	Ancient Rome	Eye Wonder
5th-8th grade	The Roman News	Andrew Langley
5th-9th grade	Is It Night or Day?: A Novel of Immigration and Survival, 1938-1942	Fern Schumer Chapman
5th-7th grade	Serafina and the Black Cloak	Robert Beatty
3rd-6th grade	Where the Mountain Meets the Moon	Grace Lin
2nd-6th grade	Your Life as an Explorer on a Viking Ship	Thomas Kingsley Troupe

Sixth Grade

Topic: Space and Exploration Non-Fiction

Essential Question: How can we prepare for the challenges of the 21st century?

TEXT COMPLEXITY	BOOK TITLE	AUTHOR
5th-8th grade	22nd Century: Future of Space	Stephanie Kuligowski
3rd-6th grade	Destination Earth	Tom Jackson
4th-6th grade	Destined for Space: Our Story of Exploration	Don Nardo
3rd-7th grade	How Do Scientists Explore Space?	Robert Snedden
3rd-7th grade	Mission to Mars	Eve Hartman
3rd-7th grade	Terrors of the Deep	Deborah Lock
3rd-6th grade	Communication (The Science Behind)	Casey Rand
3rd-7th grade	The Ultimate Adventure Atlas of Earth	National Geographic Kids
3rd-6th grade	Water is Precious	Kate McAllan
4th-7th grade	Why Is There Life on Earth?	Andrew Solway

Sixth Grade

Topic: Technology and Society Non-Fiction

Essential Question: How do great scientists find inspiration?

TEXT COMPLEXITY	BOOK TITLE	AUTHOR
3rd-7th grade	125 Cool Inventions: Supersmart Machines and Wacky Gadgets You Never Knew You Wanted!	National Geographic Kids
4th-7th grade	Ancient Science: 40 Time-Traveling, World-Exploring, History-Making Activities for Kids	Jim Wiese
4th-6th grade	Batman Science: The Real-World Science Behind Batman's Gear	Tammy Enz
2nd-6th grade	Could a Robot Make My Dinner?	Kay Barnham
2nd-6th grade	Crime-Fighting Devices	Robert Snedden
3rd-7th grade	How Come?: Every Kid's Science Questions Explained	Kathy Wollard
1st-6th grade	I Wonder Why Zippers Have Teeth	Barbara Taylor
5th-7th grade	Inside Biosphere 2: Earth Science Under Glass	Mary Kay Carson
3rd-6th grade	Isaac Newton and the Laws of Motion	Andrea Gianopoulos
3rd-6th grade	Jonas Salk and the Polio Vaccine	Katherine Krohn
6th-10th grade	Modern Medicine	Chris Oxlade
4th-7th grade	Steve Jobs	Nick Hunter
3rd-6th grade	Steve Jobs, Steve Wozniak, and the Personal Computer	Donald B. Lemke
6th-10th grade	The Impact of Technology in Sports	Matthew Anniss
1st-6th grade	The Water Cycle at Work	Rebecca Olien
3rd-6th grade	What Did the Ancient Egyptians Do For Me?	Patrick Catel

ENGAGING™ LEARNERS

Sixth Grade

Topic: Exploration Fiction

Essential Question: How can we help the people around us find courage?

TEXT COMPLEXITY	BOOK TITLE	AUTHOR
5th-7th grade	Brown Girl Dreaming	Jacqueline Woodson
5th-7th grade	The City of Ember	Jeanne DuPrau
2nd-6th grade	Dark Day in the Deep Sea	Mary Pope Osborne
2nd-6th grade	El Deafo	Cece Bell
3rd-7th grade	Escape from Mr. Lemoncello's Library	Chris Grabenstein
2nd-6th grade	Island of the Blue Dolphins	Scott O'Dell
6th-12th grade	Life of Pi	Yann Martel
3rd-7th grade	Shiloh	Phyllis Reynolds Naylor
5th-8th grade	Warriors: The New Prophecy #4: Starlight	Erin Hunter
4th-6th grade	Story Thieves	James Riley
5th-8th grade	The Tiger Rising	Kate DiCamillo
4th-8th grade	20,000 Leagues Under the Sea	Jules Verne
3rd-6th grade	The Cricket in Times Square	George Selden
4th-7th grade	From the Mixed-Up Files of Mrs. Basil E. Frankweiler	E.L. Konigsburg
6th-12th grade	Ender's Game	Orson Scott Card
6th-12th grade	In Real Life	Lawrence Tabak
3rd-6th grade	Lunch Money	Andrew Clements
6th-9th grade	The Glass Sentence	S.E. Grove
3rd-7th grade	The Hunt for Dark Infinity	James Dashner
5th-8th grade	The Journal of Curious Letters	James Dashner

Sixth Grade

Topic: Earth Systems Non-Fiction

Essential Question: What is fragile about the world we live in?

TEXT COMPLEXITY	BOOK TITLE	AUTHOR
5th-8th grade	A Long Walk to Water	Linda Sue Park
5th-8th grade	An Inconvenient Truth: The Crisis of Global Warming	Al Gore
5th-8th grade	Are Humans Damaging the Atmosphere	Catherine Chambers
1st-6th grade	Earth Smart	National Geographic Learning
4th-6th grade	How Harmful are Fossil Fuels?	Catherine Chambers
3rd-7th grade	Conservation (The Impact of Environmentalism)	Jen Green
1st-6th grade	Many Biomes, One Earth	Sneed B. Collard III
4th-6th grade	One Well: The Story of Water on Earth	Rochelle Strauss
4th-8th grade	Saving the Ghost of the Mountain: An Expedition Among Snow Leopards in Mongolia	Sy Montgomery
4th-8th grade	Creative Commons	Emily Puckett Rodgers
4th-7th grade	The Science of a Nuclear Plant Explosion	Meg Marquardt
2nd-6th grade	What If There Were No Sea Otters?: A Book About the Ocean Ecosystem	Suzanne Slade

Sixth Grade

Topic: Leadership Non-Fiction

Essential Question: How can one person make a difference in society?

TEXT COMPLEXITY	BOOK TITLE	AUTHOR
3rd-6th grade	Vote!	Eileen Christelow
2nd-6th grade	Voting	Sarah De Capua
3rd-6th grade	Voting and Elections	Michael Burgan
6th-10th grade	The American Heritage Book of Great American Speeches for Young People	Suzanne McIntire
3rd-8th grade	Elizabeth Cady Stanton: Women's Rights Pioneer	Connie Colwell Miller
5th-8th grade	Our Country's Presidents: All You Need to Know About the Presidents, From George Washington to Barack Obama	Ann Bausum
2nd-6th grade	The Story of George Washington Carver	Eva Moore
1st-6th grade	Mary McLeod Bethune	Eloise Greenfield
1st-6th grade	Nelson Mandela: Long Walk to Freedom	Chris van Wyk

Seventh Grade

Topic: Personal Courage Fiction

Essential Question: How do people find courage to stand up for their rights?

TEXT COMPLEXITY	BOOK TITLE	AUTHOR
7th-12th grade	A Raisin In the Sun	Lorraine Hansberry
6th-9th grade	A Wrinkle In Time	Madeleine L'Engle
4th-7th grade	Because of Winn-Dixie	Kate DiCamillo
3rd-8th grade	Bridge to Terabithia	Katherine Paterson
5th-8th grade	Control Under Fire	M. Zachary Sherman
5th-8th grade	Counting by 7s	Holly Goldberg Sloan
3rd-7th grade	Loser	Jerry Spinelli
3rd-7th grade	Love That Dog	Sharon Creech

Seventh Grade

Topic: Personal Courage Non-Fiction

Essential Question: What can we learn from the courage of others?

TEXT COMPLEXITY	BOOK TITLE	AUTHOR
5th-8th grade	Behind Rebel Lines: The Incredible Story of Emma Edmonds, Civil War Spy	Seymour Reit
5th-9th grade	Code Talker: A Novel About the Navajo Marines of World War Two	Joseph Bruchac
5th-8th grade	Courage Has No Color, The True Story of the Triple Nickles: America's First Black Paratroopers	Tanya Lee Stone
7th-12th grade	Fire from the Rock	Sharon Draper
4th-8th grade	Free at Last!: Stories and Songs of Emancipation	Doreen Rappaport
6th-12th grade	Great Speeches by African Americans	ed. James Daley
4th-7th grade	Heroes and She-roes: Poems of Amazing and Everyday Heroes	J. Patrick Lewis
6th-9th grade	His Name was Raoul Wallenberg	Louise Borden
5th-7th grade	I Am a Star: Child of the Holocaust	Inge Auerbacher
5th-9th grade	Navajo Code Talkers	Nathan Aaseng
4th-7th grade	Powerful Stories of Perseverance in Sports	Brad Herzog
4th-9th grade	Rosa Parks: My Story	Rosa Parks
5th-7th grade	The Underground Railroad	Raymond Bial
7th-12th grade	With Their Eyes: September 11th--The View from a High School at Ground Zero	Annie Thoms
5th-8th grade	Yes She Can!: Women's Sports Pioneers	Glenn Stout

Seventh Grade

Topic: Space Exploration Non-Fiction

Essential Question: Why is it important to explore beyond Earth?

TEXT COMPLEXITY	BOOK TITLE	AUTHOR
5th-8th grade	Cars on Mars: Roving the Red Planet	Alexandra Siy
5th-8th grade	How Do Scientists Explore Space?	Robert Snedden
5th-8th grade	Mapping Earth from Space	Robert Snedden
7th-12th grade	Mars Up Close: Inside the Curiosity Mission	Marc Kaufman
4th-8th grade	Mission to Mars	Eve Hartman
3rd-7th grade	Space Exploration	Carole Stott
6th-12th grade	Nature Guide: Stars and Planets	Robert Dinwiddie
4th-7th grade	The Man Who Went to the Far Side of the Moon: Apollo 11 Astronaut Michael Collins	Bea Uusma Schyffert
3rd-7th grade	The First Moon Landing	Gordon Purcell
3rd-7th grade	Who Was Neil Armstrong?	Roberta Edwards
4th-7th grade	Who Traveled to the Moon?	Neil Morris

Seventh Grade

Topic: Modern Technology Non-Fiction

Essential Question: What are the pros and cons of how fast technology is advancing?

TEXT COMPLEXITY	BOOK TITLE	AUTHOR
3rd-7th grade	Can You Survive Storm Chasing?	Elizabeth Raum
5th-10th grade	National Geographic Investigates: Future Tech: From Personal Robots to Motorized Monocycles	Charles Piddock
2nd-7th grade	Google Glass and Robotics Innovator Sebastian Thrun	Marne Ventura
4th-7th grade	Everything Robotics: All the Photos, Facts, and Fun to Make You Race for Robots	Jennifer Swanson
3rd-8th grade	Philo Farnsworth and the Television	Ellen S. Niz
4th-8th grade	What Are the Issues with Genetic Technology?	Eve Hartman
3rd-7th grade	Wired World	Andrew Einspruch

Seventh Grade

Topic: Sources of Conflict Fiction

Essential Question: When is it important to fight back?

TEXT COMPLEXITY	BOOK TITLE	AUTHOR
5th-8th grade	Among the Hidden	Margaret Peterson Haddix
5th-8th grade	Becoming Naomi Leon	Pam Munoz Ryan
7th-10th grade	Don't You Dare Read This, Mrs. Dunphrey	Margaret Peterson Haddix
6th-8th grade	Hatchet	Gary Paulsen
7th-9th grade	Homeboyz	Alan Lawrence Sitomer
4th-7th grade	Maniac Magee	Jerry Spinelli
2nd-7th grade	Capital Mysteries #10: The Election Day Disaster	Ron Roy
7th-10th grade	The Face on the Milk Carton	Caroline B. Cooney
6th-12th grade	True Grit	Charles Portis
7th-10th grade	Woods Runner	Gary Paulsen

Seventh Grade

Topic: Sources of Conflict Non-Fiction

Essential Question: How can we work to stop conflict before it turns into violence?

TEXT COMPLEXITY	BOOK TITLE	AUTHOR
5th-7th grade	Bad Guys and Gals of the Wild West	Dona Herweck Rice
7th-12th grade	Columbine: A True Crime Story	Jeff Kass
2nd-7th grade	Let It Begin Here!: Lexington & Concord: First Battles of the American Revolution	Dennis Brindell Fradin
3rd-7th grade	Pecos Bill, Colossal Cowboy	Sean Tulien
5th-12th grade	Pioneer Trails: Expanding & Preserving the Union	Christi E. Parker
3rd-7th grade	Ropes of Revolution: The Boston Tea Party	J. Gunderson
4th-8th grade	Which Way to the Wild West?: Everything Your Schoolbooks Didn't Tell You About Westward Expansion	Steve Sheinkin

Seventh Grade

Topic: Earth and Sky Non-Fiction

Essential Question: What makes our Earth such an ideal place for life?

TEXT COMPLEXITY	BOOK TITLE	AUTHOR
6th-8th grade	Biomes and Ecosystems	Barbara J. Davis
4th-7th grade	Earth in the Hot Seat: Bulletins from a Warming World	Marfe Ferguson Delano
3rd-8th grade	Exploring Ecosystems with Max Axiom, Super Scientist	Agnieszka Biskup
3rd-7th grade	Food Webs: Who Eats What?	Claire Llewellyn
3rd-7th grade	Geography: A Visual Encyclopedia	DK
4th-8th grade	Hurricane: Perspectives on Storm Disasters	Andrew Langley
2nd-7th grade	Ocean Food Webs in Action	Paul Fleisher
1st-7th grade	Science Chapters: Violent Weather	Andrew Collins
2nd-7th grade	Volcano: Eruption and Healing of Mt. St. Helen's	Patricia Lauber
4th-7th grade	Weather	Seymour Simon
5th-9th grade	Within Reach: My Everest Story	Mark Pfetzer

Seventh Grade

Topic: Tales of the Past Fiction

Essential Question: What can we learn from our ancestors?

TEXT COMPLEXITY	BOOK TITLE	AUTHOR
7th-10th grade	Black Storm Comin'	Diane Lee WIlson
3rd-7th grade	Caddie Woodlawn	Carol Ryrie Brink
6th-9th grade	Esperanza Rising	Pam Munoz Ryan
3rd-7th grade	Facing West: A Story of the Oregon Trail	Kathleen V. Kudlinski
4th-8th grade	Inside Out and Back Again	Thanhha Lai
5th-9th grade	Letters from Rifka	Karen Hesse
5th-8th grade	Roll of Thunder, Hear My Cry	Mildred D. Taylor
6th-10th grade	Shane	Jack Schaefer

ENGAGING LEARNERS

Seventh Grade

Topic: Tales of the Past Non-Fiction

Essential Question: Does history repeat itself?

TEXT COMPLEXITY	BOOK TITLE	AUTHOR
6th-10th grade	Beyond Courage: The Untold Story of Jewish Resistance During the Holocaust	Doreen Rappaport
5th-8th grade	Black Frontiers: A History of African American Heroes in the Old West	Lillian Schlissel
5th-8th grade	Children of the Dust Bowl: The True Story of the School at Weedpatch Camp	Jerry Stanley
7th-12th grade	One Thousand Paper Cranes: The Story of Sadako and the Children's Peace Statue	Ishii Takayuki
2nd-7th grade	Thank You Sarah: The Woman Who Saved Thanksgiving	Laurie Halse Anderson
4th-7th grade	The Birchbark House	Louise Erdrich
5th-8th grade	The Endless Steppe: Growing Up in Siberia	Esther Hautzig
5th-7th grade	The Golden Spike: How a Photograph Celebrated the Transcontinental Railroad	Don Nardo
4th-7th grade	The Oregon Trail	Mel Friedman

Seventh Grade

Topic: World Transformations

Essential Question: How do great leaders make sure their accomplishments endure?

TEXT COMPLEXITY	BOOK TITLE	AUTHOR
5th-7th grade	Breaker Boys: How a Photograph Helped End Child Labor	Michael Burgan
5th-7th grade	Daring Play: How a Courageous Jackie Robinson Transformed Baseball	Michael Burgan
7th-12 grade	Eyes Wide Open: Going Behind the Environmental Headlines	Paul Fleischman
5th-8th grade	Girls Think of Everything: Stories of Ingenious Inventions by Women	Catherine Thimmesh
6th-12th grade	Headstrong: 52 Women Who Changed Science-and the World	Rachel Swaby
6th-12th grade	I Am Malala: How One Girl Stood Up for Education and Changed the World	Malala Yousafzai
4th-8th grade	Impact: The Story of the September 11 Terrorist Attacks	Matt Doeden
3rd-7th grade	Who Was Ronald Reagan?	Joyce Milton
3rd-7th grade	Who Was Theodore Roosevelt?	Michael Burgan

Eighth Grade

Topic: Tales and Myths Fiction

Essential Question: How do mythic heroes overcome (or fail to overcome) their flaws?

TEXT COMPLEXITY	BOOK TITLE	AUTHOR
6th-12th grade	Alice's Adventures in Wonderland	Lewis Carroll
6th-9th grade	Another Pan	Daniel Nayeri and Dina Nayeri
5th-8th grade	Curse of the Thirteenth Fey: The True Tale of Sleeping Beauty	Jane Yolen
8th-12th grade	Everneath	Brodi Ashton
7th-10th grade	Greek Myths	Olivia Coolidge
5th-9th grade	The Lightning Thief	Rick Riordan
6th-10th grade	Romiette and Julio	Sharon M. Draper
5th-9th grade	The Red Pyramid	Rick Riordan
5th-8th grade	Tuck Everlasting	Natalie Babbit

Eighth Grade

Topic: Making Decisions Fiction

Essential Question: When can we be sure we've made the right choice?

TEXT COMPLEXITY	BOOK TITLE	AUTHOR
4th-8th grade	Baseball in April and Other Stories	Gary Soto
5th-8th grade	Drums, Girls and Dangerous Pie	Jordan Sonnenblick
6th-9th grade	Freak the Mighty	Rodman Philbrick
8th-12th grade	Game	Walter Dean Myers
6th-12th grade	The House on Mango Street	Sandra Cisneros
7th-12th grade	If You Come Softly	Jacqueline Woodson
7th-12th grade	Lord of the Flies	William Golding
7th-12th grade	Matched	Ally Condie
3rd-8th grade	The Big Field	Mike Lupica
7th-10th grade	The Giver	Lois Lowry
7th-10th grade	The Outsiders	S.E. Hinton
8th-10th grade	Will Grayson, Will Grayson	John Green, David Levithan

Eighth Grade

Topic: Nation of Heroes Non-Fiction

Essential Question: What is the legacy of our country?

TEXT COMPLEXITY	BOOK TITLE	AUTHOR
6th-10th grade	50 American Heroes Every Kid Should Meet	Dennis Denenberg
5th-10th grade	5,000 Miles to Freedom: Ellen and William Craft's Flight from Slavery	Dennis Fradin and Judith Fradin
7th-19th grade	The American Heritage Book of Great American Speeches for Young People	Suzanne McIntire
4th-8th grade	Choosing Courage	Peter Collier
5th-8th grade	Frederick Douglass: From Slavery to Statesman	Henry Elliot
6th-8th grade	Freedom Walkers: The Story of the Montgomery Bus Boycott	Russell Freedman
6th-9th grade	George Washington, Spymaster: How the Americans Outspied the British and Won the Revolutionary War	Thomas B. Allen
4th-8th grade	Hero of the High Seas: John Paul Jones and the American Revolution	Michael Cooper
5th-8th grade	Lincoln's Grave Robbers	Steve Sheinkin
4th-8th grade	Mary on Horseback	Rosemary Wells
3rd-8th grade	Political Leaders	Adam Sutherland
3rd-8th grade	Portraits of African-American Heroes	Tanya Bolden
7th-12th grade	Be a Changemaker: How to Start Something That Matters	Laurie Ann Thompson
8th-12th grade	Frozen in Time: An Epic Story of Survival and a Modern Quest for Lost Heroes of World War II	Mitchell Zuckoff

Eighth Grade

Topic: Famous People Non-Fiction

Essential Question: What experiences does a great leader need to have?

TEXT COMPLEXITY	BOOK TITLE	AUTHOR
5th-12th grade	Amelia Earhart	Tanya Lee Stone
3rd-8th grade	John Fitzgerald Kennedy: America's Youngest President	Lucy Post Frisbee
5th-8th grade	Elie Wiesel: Holocaust Survivor and Messenger for Humanity	Diane Dakers
4th-8th grade	Gandhi: The Young Protestor Who Founded A Nation	Philip Wilkinson
5th-8th grade	Harriet Tubman: Conductor on the Underground Railroad	Patricia Lantier
5th-10th grade	Helen Keller: A Photographic Story of a Life	Leslie Garrett
4th-8th grade	Promises to Keep: How Jackie Robinson Changed America	Sharon Robinson
3rd-8th grade	Who Was Rachel Carson	Sarah Fabiny
3rd-8th grade	You Want Women to Vote, Lizzie Stanton?	Jean Fritz

Eighth Grade

Topic: Historical Fiction

Essential Question: What can we learn from the accomplishments and setbacks of the past?

TEXT COMPLEXITY	BOOK TITLE	AUTHOR
7th-10th grade	A Death-Struck Year	Makiia Lucier
5th-9th grade	Al Capone Does My Shirts	Gennifer Choldenko
7th-12th grade	Between Shades of Gray	Ruta Sepetys
7th-12th grade	Code Talker: A Novel About the Navajo Marines of World War Two	Joseph Bruchac
4th-8th grade	Dragonwings	Laurence Yep
5th-8th grade	Forge	Laurie Halse Anderson
3rd-8th grade	Heroes Don't Run: A Novel of the Pacific War	Harry Mazer
5th-9th grade	Lyddie	Katherine Paterson
6th-8th grade	Out Of The Dust	Karen Hesse
4th-8th grade	Shades of Gray	Carolyn Reeder
4th-8th grade	The Birchbark House	Louise Erdrich
7th-10th grade	The Boy in the Striped Pajamas	John Boyne

Eighth Grade

Topic: American Poetry

Essential Question: How does the culture of the U.S.A. influence our greatest poets?

TEXT COMPLEXITY	BOOK TITLE	AUTHOR
8th-12th grade	101 Great American Poems	The American Poetry and Literacy Project
4th-8th grade	Hate That Cat	Sharon Creech
7th-12th grade	I Am the Darker Brother: An Anthology of Modern Poems by African Americans	ed. Arnold Adoff
7th-12th grade	I'm Nobody! Who Are You?	Emily Dickinson
4th-8th grade	Love That Dog	Sharon Creech
7th-12th grade	More Than Friends: Poems from Him and Her	Sara Holbrook, Allan Wolf
7th-12th grade	Robert Frost's Poems	Robert Frost
7th -12th grade	Selected Poems of E.E. Cummings	E.E. Cummings
7th-12th grade	Selected Poems of Langston Hughes	Langston Hughes

  **ENGAGING™ LEARNERS**

Eighth Grade

Topic: Space & Diseases Non-Fiction

Essential Question: What is the role of science in the 21st century?

TEXT COMPLEXITY	BOOK TITLE	AUTHOR
6th-10th grade	An American Plague: The True and Terrifying Story of the Yellow Fever Epidemic of 1793	Jim Murphy
3rd-8th grade	Comets, Asteroids and Meteors	Stuart Atkinson
6th-9th grade	Health and Disease: Investigating a TB Outbreak	Richard Spilsbury
5th-8th grade	Medieval Medicine and the Plague	Lynne Elliott
5th-8th grade	Outbreak! Plagues That Changed History	Bryn Barnard
3rd-8th grade	Miraculous Medicines (Science Solves It)	Helene Boudreau
5th-8th grade	Space, Stars, and the Beginning of Time: What the Hubble Telescope Saw	Elaine Scott
6th-8th grade	Superbugs	John DiConsiglio
3rd-8th grade	The Surprising World of Bacteria with Max Axiom, Super Scientist	Agnieszka Biskup

Eighth Grade

Topic: Scientific Advances

Essential Question: How can we prepare for all the consequences of scientific discoveries?

TEXT COMPLEXITY	BOOK TITLE	AUTHOR
4th-8th grade	1,000 Inventions and Discoveries	DK
3rd-8th grade	Jonas Salk and the Polio Vaccine	Katherine Krohn
3rd-8th grade	Louis Pasteur and Pasteurization	National Geographic Learning
5th-8th grade	Girls Think of Everything: Stories of Ingenious Inventions by Women	Catherine Thimmesh
5th-9th grade	Heroes of the Environment: True Stories of People Who Are Helping to Protect Our Planet	Harriet Rohmer
7th-12th grade	How We Got to Now: Six Innovations That Made the Modern World	Steven Johnson
3rd-8th grade	Robots at Your Service: From the Factory to Your Home	Kathryn Clay
7th-12th grade	The Next Big Thing: A History of the Boom-or-Bust Moments That Shaped the Modern World	Richard Faulk
3rd-8th grade	The Printing Press	Richard Spilsbury
3rd-8th grade	The Radio	Richard Spilsbury
3rd-8th grade	The Telephone	Richard Spilsbury
5th-9th grade	Frozen in Time: Clarence Birdseye's Outrageous Idea About Frozen Food	Mark Kurlansky
4th-8th grade	The Wildlife Detectives: How Forensic Scientists Fight Crimes Against Nature	Donna M. Jackson

Eighth Grade

Topic: Courage Fiction

Essential Question: How do brave people overcome their fears?

TEXT COMPLEXITY	BOOK TITLE	AUTHOR
8th-12th grade	1984	George Orwell
7th-10th grade	American Born Chinese	Gene Luen Yang
3rd-8th grade	Bud, Not Buddy	Christopher Paul Curtis
6th-10th grade	Chains	Laurie Halse Anderson
7th-9th grade	Code Name Verity	Elizabeth Wein
6th-9th grade	Freedom Crossing	Margaret Goff Clark
7th-10th grade	The Legend of Sleepy Hollow	Blake Hoena and Washington Irving
5th-9th grade	The Call of the Wild	Jack London
7th-12th grade	Uglies	Scott Westerfeld

ENGAGING™ LEARNERS

Ninth/Tenth Grade

Topic: Belonging

Essential Question: How does being a part of any group define an individual?

TEXT COMPLEXITY	BOOK TITLE	AUTHOR
9th-12th grade	Wolves: Behavior, Ecology, and Conservation	L. David Mech and Luigi Boitani
5th-10th grade	Though a Window: My Thirty Years with the Chimpanzees of Gombe	Jane Goodall
6th-10th grade	Fly Girls: The Forgotten Women Airforce Service Pilots of WWII	P. O'Connell Pearson
9th-12th grade	Becoming Maria: Love and Chaos in the South Bronx	Sonia Manzano
9th-12th grade	Friday Night Lights	H.G. Bissinger
7th-10th grade	Lost Names: Scenes from a Korean Boyhood	Richard E. Kim
7th-9th grade	The Outsiders	S. E. Hinton
9th-12th grade	The Perks of Being a Wallflower	Stephen Chbosky
8th-11th grade	Cat's Eye	Margaret Atwood
8th-10th grade	Black Boy	Richard Wright

Ninth/Tenth Grade

Topic: Civic Duty

Essential Question: How can an individual citizen influence governmental decision making?

TEXT COMPLEXITY	BOOK TITLE	AUTHOR
6th-9th grade	Voice of Freedom: Fannie Lou Hamer: The Spirit of the Civil Rights Movement	Carole Boston Weatherford
7th-11th grade	Wheels of Change: How Women Rode the Bicycle to Freedom (With a Few Flat Tires Along the Way)	Sue Macy
7th-10th grade	Farewell to Manzanar	Jeanne Wakatsuki Houston
10th-12th grade	Revolutionary Characters	Gordon Wood
9th-12th grade	My Dearest Friend: Letters of Abigail and John Adams	Abigail Adams & John Adams
7th-11th grade	The Gault Case: Legal Rights for Young People	Thomas J. Billitteri
5th-9th grade	Warriors Don't Cry	Melba Pattilo Beals
7th-12th grade	Miranda v. Arizona: An Individual's Rights When Under Arrest	Sue Vader Hook
8th-12th grade	Gideon's Trumpet	Anthony Lewis
10th-12th grade	America's Constitution: A Biography	Akhil Reed Amar

Ninth/Tenth Grade

Topic: Inheritance

Essential Question: How can we decide whether to follow or depart from our ancestor's examples?

TEXT COMPLEXITY	BOOK TITLE	AUTHOR
9th-12th grade	East of Eden	John Steinbeck
7th-11th grade	It Ain't All For Nothin'	Walter Dean Myers
8th-11th grade	Caramelo	Sandra Cisneros
9th-12th grade	The Poetry of Pablo Neruda	Pablo Neruda
9th-12th grade	The Joy Luck Club	Amy Tan
7th-10th grade	Yellow Raft in Blue Water	Michael Dorris
5th-9th grade	Gregor Mendel: Genetics Pioneer	Della Yannuzzi
8th-11th grade	What's in Your Genes?: From the Color of Your Eyes to the Length of Your Life, a Revealing Look at Your Genetic Traits	Katie McKissick
8th-11th grade	Extinction and Evolution: What Fossils Reveal About the History of Life	Niles Eldridge
6th-9th grade	U.S. History: People and Events: 1865-Present	George R. Lee
9th-12th grade	Evolving Animals: The Story of Our Kingdom	Wallace Arthur

Ninth/Tenth Grade

Topic: Battling Disease

Essential Question: What is a community's obligation to care for the sick and/or disabled?

TEXT COMPLEXITY	BOOK TITLE	AUTHOR
7th-10th grade	Owning It: Stories About Teens with Disabilities	ed. Donald R. Gallo
6th-9th grade	Deenie	Judy Blume
9th-12th grade	The Diary of a Superfluous Man	Ivan Turgenev
8th-11th grade	Before I Die	Jenny Downham
7th-10th grade	Deadly Invaders: Virus Outbreaks Around the World, from Marburn Fever to Avian Flu	Denise Grady
6th-10th grade	Invisible Enemies: Stories of Infectious Disease	Jeanette Farrell
9th-12th grade	The Man Who Mistook His Wife for a Hat and Other Clinical Tales	Oliver Sacks
9th-12th grade	The Ghost Map: The Story of London's Most Terrifying Epidemic--and How It Changed Science, Cities, and the Modern World	Steven Johnson
6th-10th grade	Patient Zero: Solving the Mysteries of Deadly Epidemics	Marilee Peters
5th-9th grade	Invincible Microbe: Tuberculosis and the Never-Ending Search for a Cure	Jim Murphy and Alison Bank

ENGAGING™ LEARNERS

Ninth/Tenth Grade

Topic: Ages of Exploration

Essential Question: How do new discoveries change the way humans communicate?

TEXT COMPLEXITY	BOOK TITLE	AUTHOR
9th-12th grade	The Immortal Life of Henrietta Lacks	Rebecca Skloot
8th-12th grade	E=mc2: A Biography of the World's Most Famous Equation	David Bodanis
10th-12th grade	Microbe Hunters	Paul de Kruif
6th-10th grade	Rosalind Franklin: DNA Discover	Tom Streissguth
8th-12th grade	The Right Stuff	Tom Wolfe
7th-11th grade	Women in Science: 50 Fearless Pioneers Who Changed the World	Rachel Ignotofsky
9th-12th grade	The Most Human Human: What Artificial Intelligence Teaches Us About Being Alive	Brian Christian
5th-9th grade	Breakthrough!: How Three People Saved "Blue Babies" and Changed Medicine Forever	Jim Murphy
9th-12th grade	The Road to There	Val Ross

Ninth/Tenth Grade

Topic: Founding New Enterprises

Essential Question: What is the responsibility of a founder for the projects or organizations they begin?

TEXT COMPLEXITY	BOOK TITLE	AUTHOR
9th-12th grade	Elon Musk: Tesla, SpaceX, and the Quest for a Fantastic Future	Ashlee Vance
9th-12th grade	Made to Stick: Why Some Ideas Survive and Others Die	Chip and Dan Heath
8th-11th grade	Miracle At Philadelphia: The Story of the Constitutional Convention	Catherine Drinker Bowen
6th-9th grade	The Thing About Jellyfish	Ali Benjamin
10th-12th grade	Maya's Notebook	Isabel Allende
10th-12th grade	California: Land of New Beginnings	David Lavender
7th-10th grade	Twenty Years at Hull House	Jane Addams
8th-11th grade	Ada's Algorithm: How Lord Byron's Daughter Ada Lovelace Launched the Digital Age	James Essinger
7th-10th grade	Walk on Earth a Stranger	Rae Carson
9th-12th grade	The Tempest	William Shakespeare

Ninth/Tenth Grade

Topic: Poverty

Essential Question: What must be done for the less fortunate?

TEXT COMPLEXITY	BOOK TITLE	AUTHOR
9th-12th grade	Oliver Twist	Charles Dickens
9th-12th grade	Nickel and Dimed	Barbara Ehrenreich
10th-12th grade	The Bottom Billion: Why the Poorest Countries are Failing and What Can Be Done About It	Paul Collier
7th-10th grade	The Absolutely True Diary of a Part-Time Indian	Sherman Alexie
7th-11th grade	Yours Truly	Annabel Pitcher
10th-12th grade	And Still We Rise: The Trials and Triumphs of Twelve Gifted Inner-City Students	Miles Crowin
7th-10th grade	Every Falling Star: The True Story of How I Survived and Escaped North Korea	Sungju Lee and Susan McClelland
7th-12th grade	Ten Mile River	Paul Griffin
9th-12th grade	$2.00 a Day: Living on Almost Nothing in America	Kathryn Edin
10th-12th grade	Down and Out in Paris and London	George Orwell
9th-11th grade	A Tree Grows in Brooklyn	Betty Smith

Ninth/Tenth Grade

Topic: Sustainability

Essential Question: Where can we find opportunities to balance present and future needs?

TEXT COMPLEXITY	BOOK TITLE	AUTHOR
6th-10th grade	Energy for Keeps: Creating Clean Energy from Renewable Resources	Marilyn Nemzer, Deborah Page, Anna Carter
5th-9th grade	Using STEM to Investigate Issues in Food Production	Barbara Sandall
7th-12th grade	Silent Spring	Rachel Carson
9th-12th grade	A Book of Bees	Sue Hubbell
9th-12th grade	Washed Up: The Curious Journeys of Flotsam and Jetsam	Skye Moody
6th-9th grade	John Muir: My Life With Nature	Joseph Cornell
6th-10th grade	To the Young Environmentalist	Linda Leuzzi
5th-9th grade	The Long Walk to Water	Linda Sue Park
7th-12th grade	The World Is Blue: How Our Fate and the Oceans Are One	Sylvia A. Earle
8th-11th grade	A Walk in the Woods	Bill Bryson

ENGAGING™ LEARNERS

Ninth/Tenth Grade

Topic: Transportation and Travel

Essential Question: Is traveling one of life's joys or just a means to an end?

TEXT COMPLEXITY	BOOK TITLE	AUTHOR
8th-10th grade	The Innocents Abroad	Mark Twain
9th-12th grade	Wild: From Lost to Found on the Pacific Crest Trail	Cheryl Strayed
9th-12th grade	Assassination Vacation	Sarah Vowell
5th-9th grade	The Thing About Luck	Cynthia Kadohata
9th-11th grade	What is the What	Dave Eggers
6th-9th grade	Caminar	Skila Brown
6th-10th grade	Around the World in Seventy-Two Days	Nellie Bly
10th-12th grade	The Lexus and the Olive Tree	Thomas L. Friedman
9th-12th grade	Fourteen: A Daughter's Memoir of Adventure, Sailing, and Survival	Leslie Johansen Nack
9th-12th grade	Train Wreck: The Forensics of Rail Disasters	George Bibel
8th-10th grade	The Story of the First Transcontinental Railroad: Its Projectors, Construction and History	W.F. Bailey

Eleventh/Twelfth Grade

Topic: Leaving Home

Essential Question: How do we make sure to stay true to ourselves when heading out on our own?

TEXT COMPLEXITY	BOOK TITLE	AUTHOR
9th-12th grade	Great Expectations	Charles Dickens
6th-12th grade	The Kidney Hypothetical: Or How to Ruin Your Life in Seven Days	Lisa Yee
8th-12th grade	Our Town	Thornton Wilder
9th-11th grade	Jane Eyre	Charlotte Bronte
11th-12th grade	The Left Hand of Darkness	Ursula Le Guin
9th-12th grade	The Grapes of Wrath	John Steinbeck
8th-12th grade	The Secret Side of Empty	Maria E. Andreu
9th-12th grade	The Namesake	Jhumpa Lahiri
11th-12th grade	Drown	Junot Diaz
10th-12th grade	Lucy	Jamaica Kincaid
11th-12th grade	Childe Harold's Pilgrimage	Lord Byron

Eleventh/Twelfth Grade

Topic: Surveillance and Privacy

Essential Question: What information should people have the right to keep secret?

TEXT COMPLEXITY	BOOK TITLE	AUTHOR
8th-11th grade	Little Brother	Cory Doctorow
11th-12th grade	The Minority Report	Philip K. Dick
10th-12th grade	The Circle	Dave Eggers
11th-12th grade	Pride and Prejudice	Jane Austen
11th-12th grade	The House of Mirth	Edith Wharton
8th-11th grade	Free to Fall	Lauren Miller
7th-10th grade	Teen Privacy Rights: A Hot Issue	Deanne Durrett
8th-12th grade	Most Dangerous: Daniel Ellsberg and the Secret History of the Vietnam War	Steve Sheinkin
11th-12th grade	In The Plex: How Google Thinks, Works, and Shapes Our Lives	Steven Levy
10th-12th grade	Weapons of Math Destruction: How Big Data Increases Inequality and Threatens Democracy	Cathy O'Neil

ENGAGING™
LEARNERS

Eleventh/Twelfth Grade

Topic: Artificial Intelligence

Essential Question: What roles should and shouldn't robots and A.I. play in the 21st century?

TEXT COMPLEXITY	BOOK TITLE	AUTHOR
11th-12th grade	The Society of Mind	Marvin Minsky
7th-12th grade	Robot Builder's Bonanza	Gordon McComb
10th-12th grade	Alan Turing: The Enigma	Andrew Hodges
8th-11th grade	Frankenstein	Mary Shelley
10th-12th grade	Flesh and Machines	Rodney Brooks
7th-11th grade	Speaker for the Dead	Orson Scott Card
7th-11th grade	I, Robot	Isaac Asimov
10th-12th grade	unSpun: Finding Facts in a World of Disinformation	Brooks Jackson and Kathleen Hall Jamieson
9th-12th grade	Introducing Game Theory: A Graphic Guide	Ivan Pastine and Tuvana Pastine
11th-12th grade	Superintelligence: Paths, Dangers, Strategies	Nick Bostrom
9th-12th grade	The New Cool: A Visionary Teacher, His FIRST Robotics Team, and the Ultimate Battle of Smarts	Neal Bascomb
11th-12th grade	Virtual Girl	Amy Thomson

Eleventh/Twelfth Grade

Topic: Business and Management

Essential Question: How much do personal relationships impact the business world?

TEXT COMPLEXITY	BOOK TITLE	AUTHOR
11th-12th grade	The Last Tycoon	F. Scott Fitzgerald
10th-12th grade	Dombey and Son	Charles Dickens
8th-11th grade	Fried Green Tomatoes at the Whistle Stop Cafe	Fannie Flagg
11th-12th grade	Something Happened	Joseph Heller
10th-12th grade	Rare Objects	Kathleen Tessaro
9th-12th grade	The Obstacle is the Way	Ryan Holiday
11th-12th grade	True North: Discover Your Authentic Leadership	Bill George
11th-12th grade	Thinking, Fast and Slow	Daniel Kahnemann
11th-12th grade	Reinventing the Bazaar: A Natural History of Markets	John McMillan
10th-12th grade	Grand Pursuit: The Story of Economic Genius	Sylvia Nasar

Eleventh/Twelfth Grade

Topic: The City

Essential Question: How do the realities of city living change individuals?

TEXT COMPLEXITY	BOOK TITLE	AUTHOR
8th-11th grade	Factory Girls: From Village to City in a Changing China	Leslie T. Chang
10th-12th grade	The City in Texas	David McComb
10-12th grade	Little Fish: A Memoir From A Different Kind of Year	Ramsey Beyer
9th-12th grade	Zoned in the USA: The Origins and Implications of American Land-Use Regulation	Sonia A. Hirt
11th-12th grade	The Historical Atlas of New York City: A Visual Celebration of Nearly 400 Years of New York City's History	Eric Homberger
10th-12th grade	Sister Carrie	Theodore Dreiser
10th-12th grade	Ideal Cities	Erika Meitner
9th-12th grade	Ragtime	E.L. Doctorow
11th-12th grade	Lyrics Alley	Leila Aboulela
9th-12th grade	The Amazing Adventures of Kavalier & Clay	Michael Chabon
11th-12th grade	Miami	Joan Didion

Eleventh/Twelfth Grade

Topic: Diseases of the Mind

Essential Question: To what extent are people in control of their actions?

TEXT COMPLEXITY	BOOK TITLE	AUTHOR
9th-12th grade	Still Alice	Lisa Genova
11th-12th grade	One Flew Over the Cuckoo's Nest	Ken Kesey
7th-12th grade	The Things They Carried	Tim O'Brien
9th-12th grade	Invincible	Amy Reed
7th-12th grade	The Yellow Wallpaper	Charlotte Perkins Gilman
11th-12th grade	Don Quixote	Miguel de Cervantes
11th-12th grade	Just Checking	Emily Colas
11th-12th grade	Girl, Interrupted	Susanna Kaysen
11th-12th grade	Mad in America: Bad Science, Bad Medicine, and the Enduring Mistreatment of the Mentally Ill	Robert Whitaker
9th-12th grade	50 Human Brain Ideas You Really Need to Know	Moheb Costandi
9th-12th grade	Love, Hate and Reparation	Melanie Klein and Joan Riviere
9th-12th grade	Beethoven: The Universal Composer	Edmund Morris

ENGAGING™ LEARNERS

Eleventh/Twelfth Grade

Topic: American Poetry

Essential Question: How are the American experience and the American Dream represented in our poetry?

TEXT COMPLEXITY	BOOK TITLE	AUTHOR
9th-12th grade	God's Trombones: Seven Negro Sermons in Verse	James Weldon Johnson
11th-12th grade	Lunch Poems	Frank O'Hara
10th-12th grade	The Poems of Emma Lazarus, Volume I: Narrative, Lyric, and Dramatic	Emma Lazarus
10th-12th grade	Selected Poems	Gwendolyn Brooks
9th-12th grade	The Collected Poems of Emily Dickinson	Emily Dickinson
7th-12th grade	Selected Poems	Henry Wadsworth Longfellow
11th-12th grade	Paterson	William Carlos Williams
7th-12th grade	Selected Poems	Wallace Stevens
10th-12th grade	Book of My Nights	Li-Young Lee
9th-12th grade	Collected Poems	Robert Hayden
8th-12th grade	Leaves of Grass	Walt Whitman

Eleventh/Twelfth Grade

Topic: Understanding the Universe

Essential Question: What is the value of knowing the truth?

TEXT COMPLEXITY	BOOK TITLE	AUTHOR
10th-12th grade	A Brief History of Time	Stephen Hawking
9th-12th grade	Origins: Fourteen Billion Years of Cosmic Evolution	Neil deGrasse Tyson and Donald Goldsmith
7th-11th grade	Cosmos	Carl Sagan
11th-12th grade	Galileo's Daughter	Dava Sobel
10th-12th grade	Stargazer: The Life and Times of the Telescope	Fred Watson
9th-11th grade	The Hero with a Thousand Faces	Joseph Campbell
11th-12th grade	The Day We Found the Universe	Marcia Batusiak
9th-12th grade	Siddhartha	Hermann Hesse
11th-12th grade	Star Maker	Olaf Stapledon
10th-12th grade	Bellwether	Connie Willis
11th-12th grade	The Dispossessed	Ursula Le Guin
11th-12th grade	Ficciones	Jorge Luis Borges

Eleventh/Twelfth Grade

Topic: Water

Essential Question: What is holding the world back from water being safe and abundant for everyone?

TEXT COMPLEXITY	BOOK TITLE	AUTHOR
9th-12th grade	Life of Pi	Yann Martel
11th-12th grade	Waiting for the Rain	Charles Mungoshi
11th-12th grade	Dune	Frank Herbert
10th-12th grade	In the Heart of the Sea: The Tragedy of the Whaleship Essex	Nathaniel Philbrick
9th-11th grade	Wide Sargasso Sea	Jean Rhys
11th-12th grade	Blue Revolution: Unmaking America's Water Crisis	Cynthia Barnett
7th-11th grade	The Atlas of Water: Mapping the World's Most Critical Resource	Maggie Black and Jannet King
11th-12th grade	Cadillac Desert	Marc Reisner
10th-12th grade	The End of the Line: How Overfishing is Changing the World and What We Eat	Charles Clover
7th-11th grade	The Open Ocean (Life In the Sea)	Pam Walker and Elaine Wood

APPENDIX B

Literacy & Learning Center Posters

APPENDIX B

Literacy & Learning Center Posters
CENTER NORMS POSTER

Where/how to use it: This procedure poster indicates students' four expected norms for Literacy & Learning Centers. When you're first introducing centers you should refer to the poster. Discuss each norm and emphasize why it's important. Afterwards, hang this poster prominently in the classroom as a reminder whenever you do Literacy & Learning Centers.

- **Read 3 then ask me**: Students are expected to read directions independently at each station. Teams are only to ask for help after they've attempted to answer questions themselves by reading and re-reading all available instructions at least 3 times.

- **Stay on task**: Center tasks are short and specific; students will have a limited amount of time to complete them. If students don't focus, they will find that they don't have time to finish the activities.

- **Positive language/taking care of your group**: The goal of each center is to succeed as a team. Everyone is expected to be involved and contribute his or her effort. Teammates help each other; members should avoid competing with each other.

- **Monitor your own progress**: Unlike a traditional classroom, the teacher may not be facing the students to see a raised hand – the teacher is likely to be helping others or be involved in his or her own center. Even so, assure students that you are always available to answer questions and help. Students should use the cups system (using colored cups to indicate preparedness) to communicate with the teacher. Students should not stop but instead keep working on the task if at all possible. Remind students that if they read all directions at least 3 times they may not need to ask the teacher for help.

ENGAGING™
LEARNERS

CENTER NORMS

READ 3 THEN ASK ME
Read all directions three times before asking for help.

STAY ON TASK
Focus on the task for the center.

POSITIVE LANGUAGE/ TAKING CARE OF YOUR GROUP
You're an ensemble. You take care of each other. It's your job to make your teammates look good.

MONITOR YOUR OWN PROGRESS
Use the cup system to monitor your own progress.

 **ENGAGING™ LEARNERS**

CUPS MONITORING POSTER

Where/how to use it: This procedure poster clarifies the well-known classroom strategy of using colored cups to communicate with the teacher. When you are first introducing centers you should refer to the poster, discuss the meaning of each cup color, and explain why this is a preferred method of communicating during Literacy & Learning Centers. Just like a raised hand, colored cups can be seen from anywhere in the room. But cups communicate more than a raised hand does! They allow students to proceed with their work until the teacher is able to address their concerns. Explain that during centers, the teacher needs to be free to travel the classroom to check on different groups and/or participate in a Teacher-Led Center. Assure students that the teacher will always make him or herself available to answer questions and help students as soon as possible. Hang this poster prominently in the classroom as a reminder whenever your class is doing a centers activity.

ENGAGING™ LEARNERS

CUPS MONITORING

GOOD
Put the green cup on the top of the stack if your group understands the directions and is working on the task.

STAY ON TASK
Put the yellow cup on the top of the stack if your group can get started on the task even if you have a question.

HELP
Put the red cup on the top of the stack if your group has questions and is unable to begin the task.

FINISHED
Put the blue cup on the top of the stack when your group is finished.

VOCABULARY CENTER POSTER – VOCABULARY DETECTIVES

Where/how to use it: This foundational poster explains the purpose and basic instructions for a popular vocabulary development Literacy & Learning Center activity. Hang this poster at the Vocabulary Center for student reference. At this center you'll also need to provide:

- At least 2 kinds of blank Vocabulary Detective graphic organizers

  Tip: Find Vocabulary Detective graphic organizers online, at teacher stores, or make your own. Katherine McKnight's book, *The Teacher's Big Book of Graphic Organizers* (June 2010, Jossey-Bass) contains a variety of graphic organizers that are perfect for this activity. You'll need to print plenty in order to give every student a choice!

- A completed example of each kind of graphic organizer for student reference

  Tip: Tape these examples to the desktops and/or put them in plastic sleeves so they don't "wander away" or get mixed up with student work.

- Detailed instructions

  Tip: Handwrite or type clear instructions indicating how many words each group is expected to investigate and where they will get the words – for example they can choose them from a provided list, draw them from a 'hat', or choose them independently from their texts. Depending on your class and the graphic organizers you choose to offer, you may also want to provide definitions of words like synonym, antonym, parts of speech, etc. Students may also need access to glossaries or dictionaries (either print or online). You know your students better than anyone else, so you're the best one to decide how many words can be investigated during a given amount of time and how much support your students need. Tape instructions to the desktops and/or put them in plastic sleeves so they don't "wander away."

  ENGAGING™ LEARNERS

VOCABULARY DETECTIVES

The center instructions will tell you how many words you're investigating today.

CHOOSE one style of graphic organizer for each word. They can all be the same or you can mix them up!

READ instructions for each graphic organizer. Look at a completed example if you need further explanation.

REMEMBER to fill in your name on the top of each completed graphic organizer.

ENGAGING™ LEARNERS

VOCABULARY CENTER POSTER – CONCEPT SORT

Where/how to use it: This foundational poster explains the purpose and basic instructions for a popular vocabulary development Literacy & Learning Center activity. Hang this poster at the Vocabulary Center for student reference. At this center you'll also need to provide:

- A stack of 10 or more vocabulary words or terms, written on index cards.

- Blank slips of paper and pencils/pens for students to write their categories.

- Detailed instructions.

Tip: Handwrite or type clear instructions indicating if students are allowed to use glossaries/dictionaries, or if they're allowed to refer to their texts for context clues, during this activity. You know your students better than anyone else, so you're the best one to decide how many words or terms are relevant to each particular text and how much support your students need. Tape instructions to the desktops and/or put them in plastic sleeves so they don't "wander away."

ENGAGING™ LEARNERS

CONCEPT SORT

Each index card shows one term or concept from our reading material.

1 As a team, briefly **DISCUSS** each term's meaning.

2 Work together to **SORT** all terms into categories based on their meanings. You can write your categories on the blank slips of paper. Try to come up with categories that don't leave any words "left over".

3 Discuss your reasoning and **EXPLAIN**:
- How did you choose your categories?
- How did you decide which word or term belongs in each category?

ENGAGING™
LEARNERS

READING TOGETHER CENTER POSTER - VISUALIZATION

Where/how to use it: Visualization, or creating a mental picture, is a powerful comprehension skill that empowers student readers to tackle increasingly difficult texts. This foundational poster offers students an opportunity to read a text, create a visual image, and then share that visualization with others. Hang this poster at the Reading Together Center for student reference. At this center you'll need to provide:

- A text that's appropriate for illustration.

  Tip: This can be informational text that is relevant to your classroom studies or it can be an excerpt from a piece of fiction, drama or poetry. Ideally, you'll let the student choose his or her own excerpt from a book or article that he/she is reading independently.

- Art supplies like paper, colored pencils, markers, etc. OR computers with illustration software or internet access.

- Detailed instructions.

  Tip: Handwrite or type clear instructions including where students are to access the text: print-outs of a preselected text can be provided, students can be referred to a page of a classroom text, or students can be encouraged to choose a selection on their own. You know your students and your curriculum better than anyone else so you're the best one to decide what would be most useful. Content-area teachers, for example, might want students to illustrate scientific concepts, historic events, or technical procedures. ELA teachers might want students to illustrate events or settings from a novel. If you prefer that students create digital illustrations, instructions should include details about which program, website, etc. they should use. Confirm that everyone is familiar with the software before beginning centers. Tape instructions to the desktops and/or put them in plastic sleeves so they don't "wander away."

ENGAGING™ LEARNERS

VISUALIZATION

Successful readers create mental pictures as they read. In this center you'll have an opportunity to draw an illustration of what you picture in your head.

READ a scene, paragraph, or section from a text. The center instructions will tell you what text to use.

CREATE an illustration for the selected text. Include as much detail as possible. Feel free to label elements of the illustration if necessary, but try to create it in such a way that it can be understood without the use of words.

SHARE your illustration with your teammates

ENGAGING™
LEARNERS

READING TOGETHER CENTER POSTER - DRTA (DIRECTED READING AND THINKING ACTIVITY)

Where/how to use it: Before-, during-, and after-reading activities help student readers take an active approach to texts.

This foundational poster includes general instructions for a popular Directed Reading and Thinking Activity (DRTA). Hang this poster at the Reading Together Center for student reference. At this center you'll need to provide:

- A text (literature or informational text).

  Tip: Ideally this would be a "just right" text of the student's own choosing.

- Blank 3-column graphic organizers.

  Tip: Find printable 3-column graphic organizers online, at teacher stores, or make your own. Katherine McKnight's books, *Common Core Literacy for ELA, History/Social Studies*, and the *Humanities: Strategies to Deepen Content Knowledge (Grades 6-12)* (April 2014, Jossey-Bass) and *Common Core Literacy for Math, Science, and Technical Subjects: Strategies to Deepen Content Knowledge (Grades 6-12)* (October 2014, Jossey-Bass) contain reproducible DRTA graphic organizers. Make sure you print at least one for each student.

- An example of a completed DRTA form for student reference.

  Tip: The first time you introduce the activity you may find it helpful to model the DRTA steps as a mini-lesson before beginning centers. Tape the completed example to the desktops and/or put it in a plastic sleeve so it doesn't "wander away" or get mixed up with student work.

- Detailed instructions.

  Tip: Handwrite or type instructions indicating which text students should use.

ENGAGING™ LEARNERS

DRTA:
DIRECTED READING AND THINKING ACTIVITY

This activity will help you practice being a more active reader.

PREVIEW

In the first column, write what you think the text is going to be about **BEFORE** you read it.
What will the author's main points be? Look for clues: are there illustrations or headings? If you've read an earlier part of this text, do you remember what it said? How might the author continue?

TAKE NOTES

In the second column, take notes **WHILE** you read the text. What are the author's main points?

REVIEW

AFTER you're done reading, use the last column for writing down the ways in which your preview was correct *and* the ways in which the text surprised you.

ENGAGING™
LEARNERS

WRITER'S CRAFT CENTER POSTER – QUESTIONING THE AUTHOR

Where/how to use it: This foundational poster offers students an opportunity to read a text and then express what they've learned in their own words. Hang this poster at the Writer's Craft Center for student reference. At this center you'll need to provide:

- An appropriate text at least one paragraph long.

  Tip: Make sure that the text includes atleast one main point and one or more supporting points. It can be informational text that is relevant to your classroom studies or it can be an excerpt from a piece of fiction or poem that your class has been reading. You know your students and your classroom, so be sure to select a text that is appropriately challenging.

- Paper and pens/pencils OR access to computers and word processing software.

- Detailed instructions.

  Tip: Handwrite or type clear instructions indicating if students are allowed to use glossaries, dictionaries, style guides, or other reference material in order to compose their best writing. You'll also need to indicate how much students are expected to write. In some classrooms students may need practice in answering questions with complete sentences; some students may be learning to craft full paragraphs. You know your students better than anyone else, so you're the best one to decide how much your students can be expected to write and how much support they need. Tape instructions to the desktops and/or put them in plastic sleeves so they don't "wander away."

ENGAGING™
LEARNERS

QUESTIONING THE AUTHOR

1 Read the text **AS A GROUP**.

2 Each team member should **INDEPENDENTLY** write an answer to the following question. Use your own words.
What is the author's main point?

3 Then each member should **INDEPENDENTLY** write an additional answer to **ONE** of the following questions. You don't all have to choose the same question.
Why do you think the author might be telling you this?

How does the author support his or her main point?

How is the author's point of view relevant to you personally?

What else would you like to know about this?

4 If you have time, **AS A GROUP**, proofread each other's work. Check for correct spelling, punctuation, sentence structure, etc.

ENGAGING™ LEARNERS

TEACHER-LED CENTER POSTER

Where/how to use it: This foundational poster explains the purpose of the Teacher-Led Literacy & Learning Center. The Teacher-Led Center provides the opportunity for students to meet with the teacher and to go over a particular skill. In addition, this center can provide the opportunity for teachers to assess a student's understanding or mastery of a skill. This center can also be used for interventions. While the purpose for this center can be different from one day to the next, the teacher should always state a clear purpose and make sure that students understand the center's goal.

TEACHER-LED CENTER

Here's your chance to meet with the teacher to:

WORK on a skill

ASK a question

DEMONSTRATE what you know

LEARN something new

OR

SHARE your thoughts

ENGAGING™ LEARNERS

READING WITH A PLAN POSTER

Where/how to use it: This deep reading poster clarifies 8 strategies that successful readers use when they encounter difficult text. Refer to this poster when you introduce deep reading centers. Explain each strategy. Give the students an opportunity to discuss which strategies they already use, which ones have proven to be most useful, and which ones they'd like to try. Afterwards, hang this poster prominently in the classroom as a reminder – it will be helpful whenever students do independent reading and when you do classroom Literacy & Learning Centers. Consider modeling these strategies whenever you read aloud to the class.

- **Before You Read Strategies:** To expand upon the strategies listed on the poster, teachers can offer content-specific Anticipation Guides that encourage students to reinforce and build upon prior knowledge. And they can encourage students to scan text for new or interesting vocabulary words.

- **While You Read Strategies**: In addition to the strategies listed, urge students to ask questions as they read. They can write them down in a "reading diary", use sticky notes in the text margins, or verbalize while reading aloud with peers.

- **After You Read Strategies**: In addition to the before- and after- reading strategies on the poster, remind students that they can use post reading strategies to help make sure the information "sticks." Common after-reading strategies include summarizing, discussing text with others, and writing or verbalizing a critique of the text.

ENGAGING™ LEARNERS

READING WITH A PLAN

BEFORE YOU READ

PREVIEW - Get a sense of a text before you start. For example: look for clues in the title, skim opening paragraphs, and check out illustrations.

PREDICT - Guess what will happen.

SET A PURPOSE - Decide why you are reading. For example: are you trying to answer a question, be entertained, or learn new information about a particular topic?

USE PRIOR KNOWLEDGE - Jot down things you already know about this topic.

WHILE YOU READ

VISUALIZE - Create a mental picture.

CONNECT - Relate personally to what you read. For example: does the text remind you of anything in your own life?

MONITOR - Check your comprehension as you go. Re-read difficult passages or ask for help if necessary.

MAKE INFERENCES - Look for evidence in the text and use it to draw logical conclusions.

ENGAGING™ LEARNERS

READING TOGETHER CENTER POSTER - TEXT-THINK-CONNECT

Where/how to use it: This deep reading poster explains the purpose and basic instructions for a popular after-reading Literacy & Learning Centers activity. It provides a three-part approach for analyzing and reflecting on a text. Hang this poster at the Reading Together Center for student reference. At this center you'll also need to provide:

- Various 3-column graphic organizers, blank paper for students who prefer to make their own, and pens/pencils.

- Copies of the text to be analyzed.

- Detailed instructions.

  Tip: Handwrite or type clear instructions indicating which text you want students to analyze. Ideally, this should be text that the students have already read. If possible, let them choose between a few different texts; these can be different sections of a textbook chapter, supplemental reading material, or a text that you've written yourself. Indicate if students are to work independently or in teams.

TEXT · THINK · CONNECT

READ the center instructions carefully **TO LEARN**:

1. what text, story or book you're analyzing

2. if you're working individually, in pairs, or as a group

CHOOSE a graphic organizer **OR CREATE** your own 3-column grid.

1. In the first column: record your favorite direct quotes from the **TEXT**.

2. In the second column: **THINK** about the quotes you picked. Try to figure out how each quote relates to the author's main point, or guess why the author chose those exact words.

3. In the third column: record your personal connections with the text. Good readers **CONNECT** texts to their personal experiences, knowledge and beliefs.

ENGAGING™
LEARNERS

READING TOGETHER CENTER POSTER - STORY TRAILS/SEQUENCING

Where/how to use it: Many texts - both literature and informational - include sequential steps. This deep reading poster clarifies the thought process involved in identifying those sequential steps. It may be helpful to model the skill of identifying sequential steps for your students, so be prepared to offer a mini-lesson in identifying "clue words" like: first, initially, next, then, eventually, meanwhile, so, finally, etc. Hang this poster at the Reading Together Center for student reference. At this center you'll also need to provide:

- Various story trail or sequencing graphic organizers, blank paper for students who prefer to make their own, and pens/pencils.

- Copies of the text to be analyzed.

- Detailed instructions.

  Tip: Handwrite or type clear instructions indicating which text you want students to analyze. Make sure the text includes sequential steps! ELA teachers may consider having students analyze a section of fiction or poetry that includes various plot points like a chase scene or escalating confrontation, for example. Content-area teachers can offer text that explains procedures, historical events, game rules, etc. Indicate if students are to work independently or in teams.

ENGAGING™ LEARNERS

STORY TRAILS/SEQUENCING

IDENTIFY the suggested number of key events in the text. Be prepared to explain why you think each event is important.

CHOOSE one style of graphic organizer or use blank paper and create your own.

READ instructions on the graphic organizer. Look at a completed example if you need further explanation.

PUT important events in the correct order, completing the graphic organizer as instructed.

ENGAGING™ LEARNERS

READING TOGETHER CENTER POSTER - INDEPENDENT READING WITH STICKY NOTES

Where/how to use it: This deep reading poster is perfect for use at a Reading Together Center where each student reads a book or article of his/her own choosing. It can work in tandem with the READING WITH A PLAN poster, encouraging students to select strategies they find most useful, or with any strategy you want them to practice. Hang this poster at the Reading Together Center for student reference. At this center you'll need to provide:

- Texts for independent reading.

- Sticky notes and pens/pencils.

- Detailed instructions.

    Tip: Handwrite or type clear instructions indicating if you want students to work on a particular reading strategy or giving them permission to choose their own.

INDEPENDENT READING
WITH STICKY NOTES

READ your text INDEPENDENTLY.

Use the provided sticky notes to record **QUESTIONS**, **COMMENTS**, and personal **CONNECTIONS** in the margins of the text.

Before you start:
READ the center instructions **CAREFULLY** to see if you're supposed to be looking for anything **SPECIFIC**!

READING TOGETHER CENTER POSTER – PLOT ANALYSIS

Where/how to use it: Literature and humanities teachers are familiar with dozens of plot analysis activities. This deep reading poster is purposefully ambiguous so that you can adapt your favorites to use as Literacy & Learning Centers. Hang this poster at the Reading Together Center for student reference. At this center you'll need to provide:

- A literature text.

  Tip: Ideally this would be a "just right" text of the student's own choosing.

- An assortment of blank graphic organizers

  Tip: Find printable plot analysis graphic organizers online, at teacher stores, or make your own. Katherine McKnight's book, *Common Core Literacy for ELA, History/Social Studies, and the Humanities: Strategies to Deepen Content Knowledge* (Grades 6-12) (April 2014, Jossey-Bass) contains many examples like: Questioning the Author, Story Trails, Literary Letters, and Character Questionnaire. Her book, *The Teacher's Big Book of Graphic Organizers: 100 Reproducible Organizers that Help Kids with Reading, Writing, and the Content Areas* includes reproducible graphic organizers including many to strengthen reading comprehension. Wherever you get them, make sure you get enough so each student has a choice.

- An example of completed graphic organizers for student reference.

  Tip: The first time you introduce the activity you may find it helpful to model each graphic organizer as a mini-lesson before beginning centers. Tape the completed example to the desk tops and/or put it in a plastic sleeve so it doesn't "wander away" or get mixed up with student work.

- Detailed instructions.

  Tip: Handwrite or type instructions indicating which text students should use and advising them if they should work independently or as a team.

ENGAGING™ LEARNERS

PLOT ANALYSIS

READ THE CENTER INSTRUCTIONS carefully to learn:

- What text, story or book you're analyzing

- If you're working individually, in pairs or as a group

CHOOSE a **PLOT ANALYSIS ACTIVITY** to complete.

ENGAGING™ LEARNERS

LISTENING CENTER POSTER – QCC (QUESTIONS, COMMENTS, AND CONNECTIONS)

Where/how to use it: This Listening Center poster offers students a "game plan" for developing active listening skills. You may want to model these listening skills in a mini-lesson. It may also be helpful to point out that active listening and deep reading employ many of the same skills; developing one can help develop the other. At this center you'll need to provide:

- An audio recording (or selection of audio recordings) of content-related material.

  Tip: These can be excerpts from interviews with experts, podcasts, lectures – or you can record yourself reading a text of your choosing. Recordings can be played on any mp3 players, CD players, or even tape recorders. Many teachers find it helpful to have students provide their own earphones/earbuds for this purpose.

- Paper and pens/pencils.

- Detailed instructions.

  Tip: Handwrite or type instructions indicating what recording students should listen to – or specifying if you want them to choose between recordings.

LISTENING QCC
QUESTION COMMENTS AND CONNECTIONS

This activity will help you practice being a more active listener.

1 Individually "take notes" while you listen to the passage. They don't have to be neat or easy to read; they're just for you. These notes can be:

QUESTIONS things you want to know more about or don't understand

COMMENTS your thoughts about what you're hearing

CONNECTIONS ways in which the passage relates to your life or things that you already know about

2 When everyone is done, share your notes as a group. Don't be surprised if everyone in your group has different questions, comments, and connections!

ENGAGING™ LEARNERS

GRAMMAR CENTER POSTER – STOPPING RUN-ONS

Where/how to use it: This Grammar Center poster reminds students of the importance of clearly written communication in all subject areas. It also encourages them to read important content closely, paying attention to the meaning of each individual sentence. Hang this poster at the Grammar Center for student reference. At this center you'll also need to provide:

- Blank paper and pencils/pens.

- Sample texts that include run-on sentences. You can write these yourself, adapt them from texts that relate to your content, or re-write texts that your students are already studying. For example, choose a passage from a textbook and rewrite it to include run-on sentences.

  Tip: If you're unsure of what a run-on sentence is, check out any grammar website. I especially like Mignon Fogarty (Grammar Girl) for her simple, no-nonsense tips and easy-to-understand explanations. www.quickanddirtytips.com/education/grammar/what-are-run-on-sentences

- Detailed instructions.

  Tip: Handwrite or type clear instructions indicating which sample texts the student teams should analyze. If possible, offer a choice of texts and let them choose. If the text includes new or recently introduced vocabulary, students may also need access to glossaries or dictionaries (either print or online). Tape instructions to the desktops and/or put them in plastic sleeves so they don't "wander away."

ENGAGING™ LEARNERS

STOPPING RUN-ONS

1 Read each text **AS A GROUP.**

2 **IDENTIFY** the run-on sentences and discuss how they could be re-written correctly.

HINTS:

LOOK for conjunctions (words like *and*, *but*, or *so*).

LOOK for ideas that are "smashed together" without punctuation.

DISCUSS where you would want to breathe if you read the passage aloud.

3 Work together to **REWRITE** the text using clear, simple sentences.

ENGAGING™ LEARNERS

WRITER'S CRAFT CENTER POSTER – R.A.F.T.

Where/how to use it: New standards expect students to respond to the varying demands of audience, task, purpose and discipline. Use this Writer's Craft Center poster at a center that gives students an opportunity to adapt their writing to various roles, audiences, formats and tasks. Hang this poster at the center for reference. At this center you'll also need to provide:

- Blank paper and pencils/pens or computers with word processing software.

- Detailed instructions.

  Tip: Handwrite or type clear instructions. Tape instructions to the desktops and/or put them in plastic sleeves so they don't "wander away."

This center requires you to be creative and plan in advance. Decide what role, audience, format, and task would be most helpful and relevant to your content. Remember, the student's role and the audience can belong to any real or imagined group. Search online or see Katherine McKnight's *Common Core Literacy* (2014, Jossey-Bass) books for ideas that will get you started. If possible, have a variety of options and allow students to select their favorite.

R. A. F. T.

As a good writer, you'll vary your writing style depending on 4 things:

Role
Who are you?

Audience
Who are you writing to?

Format
What are you writing?
(letter, tweet, blog post, poem, etc.)

Topic
What are you writing about?

1 **READ** the center instructions carefully as a group.

2 **WRITE** your piece as instructed. Remember to put your real name somewhere on your work!

ENGAGING™ LEARNERS

Wish you had an experienced coach by your side as your team implements Literacy & Learning Centers?

Let us assist in your classroom

Contact us at
info@EngagingLearners.com
or call **(312) 576-8222**

to schedule a free, no-obligation phone consultation with Dr. McKnight

The Engaging Learners team can come to YOU!

Sometimes modeling is the best way to help teachers see the power of Literacy & Learning Centers. We work with school leadership to create customized professional development that addresses each school's unique challenges – including hands on work in your classrooms. Join us as we prepare your students to achieve amazing literacy growth. Visit **www.EngagingLearners.com/on-site** for more info.

APPENDIX C

Resources for Centers

APPENDIX C
Resources for Centers

Teacher-Led Centers

Flexible Grouping

An excellent example to provide differentiated instruction through student self-reflection and evaluation.
https://www.teachingchannel.org/videos/guided-groups-formative-assessment#

Formative Assessment Tools

This article lists 55 digital tools for formative assessment.
https://www.nwea.org/blog/2016/take-three-55-digital-tools-and-apps-for-formative-assessment-success/

Providing Meaningful Feedback to Students

"5 Research-Based Tips for Providing Students with Meaningful Feedback" from Edutopia outlines the most effective strategies for descriptive feedback.
https://www.edutopia.org/blog/tips-providing-students-meaningful-feedback-marianne-stenger

Using Formative Reading Assessment to Enhance Content Area Learning

In this webinar, the presenters share practical tools to gather information about students as readers and instructional responses that promote increased understanding of subject matter. These tools and strategies can be implemented at the Teacher-Led Center.
http://iste.adobeconnect.com/p3zymmdedcw/

Reading Together Centers

In addition to the book lists in Appendix A, the following sites also provide resources for text differentiation.

NewsELA

A website differentiates texts based on Lexile score. **Newsela.com**

Comprehension Game Trio: Cause and Effect, Fact or Opinion & Context Clues (Grades 4-5)

From **ReallyGoodStuff.com**, "Use any of three card decks with any of three fun board games to practice key comprehension skills. Each deck has 50 brief yet substantial passages with multiple-choice questions. Differentiate by skill, game board, literature/informational text, and independent reading levels; the dice icons on the cards indicate complexity, and slides, ladders, and bonuses add excitement."

Comprehension Cubes

From **ReallyGoodStuff.com**. "Attack multiple comprehension and speaking and listening standards with this fun activity. Children roll, verbally respond, and then record their answers to the cubes' standards-based, text dependent questions. This set includes 2 literature cubes and 2 informational text cubes."

QUIZMO® Structural Skills Game

A game that is helpful for students who are having challenges with decoding and sounding out words. "Familiarize students with base words and affixes with this Bingo-style game. The game boards feature base (root) words on one side and affixes (prefixes and suffixes) on the other. Students will improve their ability to divide words into syllables, recognize multisyllabic words, and develop vocabulary as they determine whether their cards contain the bases and affixes called out by the teacher."

Teaching Points™ Comprehension Clips: Grades 4-6

"These time-saving, color-coded by- skill clips, each with a standards-based teaching point and question. Simply slip the clips onto any text for interactive read aloud, written response, and assessment. Higher-order questions boost confidence in the caliber of your questioning as you teach metacognition and critical thinking. Skill areas include Author's Purpose, Context Clues, Determine Importance, Fluency, Infer, Integrate Information, Literary Features, Questioning, Synthesize, and Text Features. Guide features at-a-glance numbered lists of 120 teaching points, skills, and strategies." These are available at **ReallyGoodStuff.com**.

Stop 'N' Jot 6-In-1 Poster Set and Study Stickies Kit

"Designed for the gradual release model of instruction, this kit includes six dry erase mini posters that match our Stop 'N' Jot Study Stickies. Before reading, demonstrate finding and recording textual evidence on mini posters. During reading, students record their thinking on Study Stickies. After reading and discussion, share students' best responses. The kit targets standards in Comprehension, Writing, Language, and Speaking & Listening." This kit could be used at the Reading Together, Writer's Craft, Vocabulary, or Speaking & Listening Center The kit is available at **ReallyGoodStuff.com**.

Inferences Mission Kit

Inferential reading is challenging, especially as students work with complex texts. From **ReallyGoodStuff.com**, "Tuck one of the 16 entertaining scenario cards into the envelope, and send your class or a group of students on a mission. Along the way, they must follow clues, make inferences, and provide evidence to support their conclusions."

Vocabulary Centers

In addition to graphic organizers, games are a valuable resource for the development of language and vocabulary. I have used the following games with students in 4th-12th grade. I found the following games on **ReallyGoodStuff.com**.

QUIZMO® Analogies Game

"Teach the principle behind analogies and show how two-word pairs are logically related with this Bingo-style game. It features five different types of analogies and over 200 individual analogies at two different levels of play. Students will build language skills, auditory memory skills, test-taking skills, and more as they determine the word that completes the analogy. Two to 36 players." These are available at **ReallyGoodStuff.com**.

Figurative Language in a Jar

A card based activity where students can explore similes, metaphors, and idiomatic expressions. This is available at **ReallyGoodStuff.com**. This activity could be used at the Writer's Center, Figurative Language/Literary Devices center.

Writer's Craft

Story Prompt Sticks

From **ReallyGoodStuff.com**, "With thousands of possible combinations, students will never be at a loss for story ideas with these creative, color-coded sticks. They simply pick one blue stick (character), one purple stick (action), and one green stick (setting), and they're ready to write!"

Task, Purpose, And Audience Write-Abouts Flip Book

From **ReallyGoodStuff.com**, "Students can generate thousands of great writing starters as they flip through these pages to choose a writing task, a reason for writing it, and an audience for that writing."

Sadlier Publishing

Sadlier Publishing (**http://www.sadlier.com/school/resources**) has free online resources that are readily adaptable for centers. Here are some examples for the Writer's Craft Center.

33 Journal Writing Prompts (Grades 6-12)
https://goo.gl/YFKsyn

Opinion Piece Writing Outline Graphic Organizer (Grades 3-8)
https://goo.gl/OnkY8f

Social Media Quick Write
https://goo.gl/4s8bi3

Letter Writing Prompt Activity
https://goo.gl/CTsLOl

Editing Activity
https://goo.gl/odnuGG

Translating Shakespeare Writing Activity (Grades 9-12)
https://goo.gl/PQAUNl

Write to a Prompt Activity (Grades 9-12)
https://goo.gl/ofYppX

ENGAGING™ LEARNERS

Other Resources and Websites for Reading Comprehension

All About Adolescent Literacy

A comprehensive website, focusing on research and classroom strategies to promote reading skills in teenagers. The Classroom Strategies section contains reading, writing and vocabulary strategies with accompanying printables.

Plastic Sleeves

Use plastic sleeves for text annotation. The text, a book or printed sheet, can be inserted into the sleeve and the student can use dry erase markers to annotate and mark up text.

Other Resources from Katherine McKnight, PhD

Books

McKnight, Katherine S. (2019). *Literacy & Learning Centers: Content Area and Disciplinary Literacy Tools for Grades 4-12 (Volume 1)*. Antioch, IL

McKnight, Katherine S. (2013). The Elementary Teacher's Big Book of Graphic Organizers K-5: 100+ Ready-to-Use

McKnight, Katherine S. (2013). *The Elementary Teacher's Big Book of Graphic Organizers K-5:* 100+ Ready-to-Use Organizers That Help Kids Learn Language Arts, Science, Social Studies, and More. San Francisco, CA: Jossey-Bass.

McKnight, Katherine S. (2010). *The Teacher's Big Book of Graphic Organizers: 100 Reproducible Organizers That Help Kids with Reading, Writing, and the Content Areas*. San Francisco, CA: Jossey-Bass.

Engaging Learners Professional Development

A website with activities and lessons for centers that is geared for grades 4-12. **EngagingLearners.com/ professional-development**

Engaging Learners Tools

A website with activities and lessons for centers that is geared for grades 4-12. **EngagingLearners.com/tools**

Want more classroom activities?

**Literacy & Learning Centers:
Content Area and Disciplinary Literacy Tools
for Grades 4-12, Volume 1**

This book is comprised of some of the most popular, downloadable activities from the LITERACY & LEARNING CENTERS RESOURCES subscription website. It includes teacher-tested activities that have been specifically designed for use with the Literacy & Learning Centers model – but they can be used in any classroom!

Available on katherinemcknight.com and Amazon!

For rates on bulk order contact **info@engaginglearners.com**.

APPENDIX D
Graphic Organizers

APPENDIX D
Graphic Organizers

Graphic organizers are important and effective tools for organizing content and ideas. They make it easy for learners to comprehend and remember new information and they are particularly useful to students whose preferred learning style requires a lot of mental spatial arrangement.

See completed examples of these graphic organizers and handouts, or get ideas for using them, here:

Vocabulary Slide
Chapter 3:
The Foundational Centers
(Vocabulary Center)

List-Group-Label
Chapter 3:
The Foundational Centers
(Vocabulary Center)

Cornell Notes
Chapter 3:
The Foundational Centers
(Reading Together Center)

GIST
Chapter 3:
The Foundational Centers
(Reading Together Center)

Evidence Based Written Argument
Chapter 3:
The Foundational Centers
(Writer's Craft Center)

Panel of Experts
Chapter 3:
The Foundational Centers
(Writer's Craft Center)

Sequence of Events
Chapter 4:
Beyond the Foundational
Centers (ELA Key Events)

Story Trails
Chapter 4:
Beyond the Foundational
Centers (ELA Key Events)

Commonly Used Prepositions
Chapter 4:
Beyond the Foundational
Centers (ELA Grammar)

  ENGAGING™ LEARNERS

You have permission to reprint these for your own classroom use but don't stop there! Because student choice is so important, it's a good idea to let student teams choose from a variety of graphic organizers and complete their chosen one in the Literacy & Learning Center. Of course you can purchase or download graphic organizers from many sources but it's not difficult to create your own. The art options in your favorite word processing software make it easy to create neat graphic organizers that are custom-designed for any classroom application. And don't be shy about letting students draw their own graphic organizers. As their close reading skills grow, they can decide which graphic representation best expresses the author's organization scheme for a particular text.

© 2019 Engaging Learners, LLC

VOCABULARY SLIDE

People in your Group: _____

Date: _____

Synonym

Picture or icon of vocabulary word

Antonymn

Vocabulary word

Part of speech

Sentence using the vocabulary word

You have permission to reproduce this page for use in your classroom.

ENGAGING™ LEARNERS

LIST- GROUP- LABEL

People in your Group: _____

Date: _____

Write down the words, phrases, and concepts that were brainstormed. Include ones that you already knew.

Categories

CORNELL NOTES

People in your Group: _____

Date: _____

Topic:

Key Points:

Supporting Points/Details:

Summary:

You have permission to reproduce this page for use in your classroom.

  **ENGAGING™ LEARNERS**

GIST

People in your Group: _____

Date: _____

Title of Reading Selection :

Directions : Preview the reading selection. Write down the key words and phrases. Then write a 20-word summary sentence using as many of the keywords as you can.

Key words and phrases :

20-word summary sentence :

You have permission to reproduce this page for use in your classroom.

EVIDENCE BASED WRITTEN ARGUMENT

People in your Group: _____

Date: _____

What is the author's claim?:

What key points did the author use to support the claim?

Point #1

    Yes No

☐ ☐ Does this point support the claim?

☐ ☐ Is this point convincing/believable? Why or why not?

_____

_____

_____

Point #2

    Yes No

☐ ☐ Does this point support the claim?

☐ ☐ Is this point convincing/believable? Why or why not?

_____

_____

_____

Point #3

    Yes No

☐ ☐ Does this point support the claim?

☐ ☐ Is this point convincing/believable? Why or why not?

_____

_____

_____

What is this reader's conclusion?

Do you think the key points provide enough evidence to support the author's claim? Explain:

_____

_____

_____

_____

You have permission to reproduce this page for use in your classroom.

  **ENGAGING™ LEARNERS**

PANEL OF EXPERTS

People in your Group: _____

Date: _____

As you watch Panel of Experts, record the different points of view that are represented. Record corresponding details and information for each point of view. Use this information to draft a written summary of the presented information.

	Name of Expert	What is their viewpoint?	What details and evidence does the expert provide to support their viewpoint?
Expert One			
Expert Two			
Expert Three			
Expert Four			

You have permission to reproduce this page for use in your classroom.

SEQUENCE OF EVENTS

People in your Group:_____

Date: _____

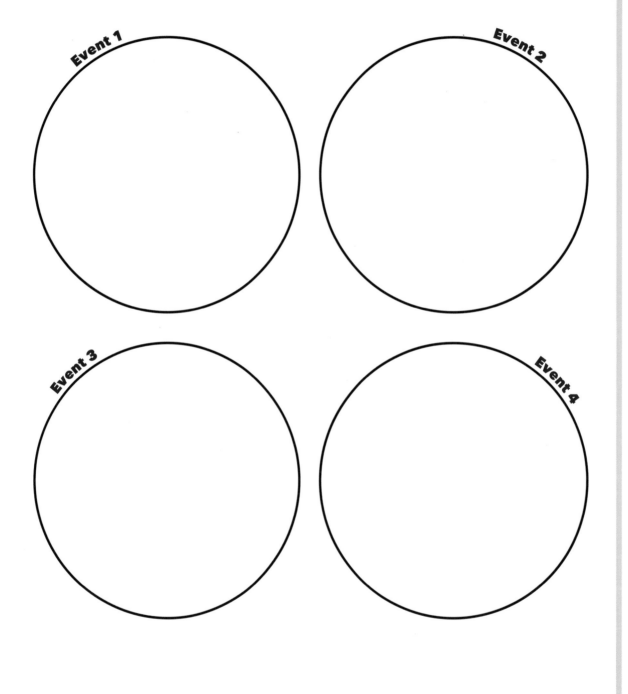

Event 1

Event 2

Event 3

Event 4

You have permission to reproduce this page for use in your classroom.

ENGAGING™ LEARNERS

STORY TRAILS

People in your Group: _____

Date: _____

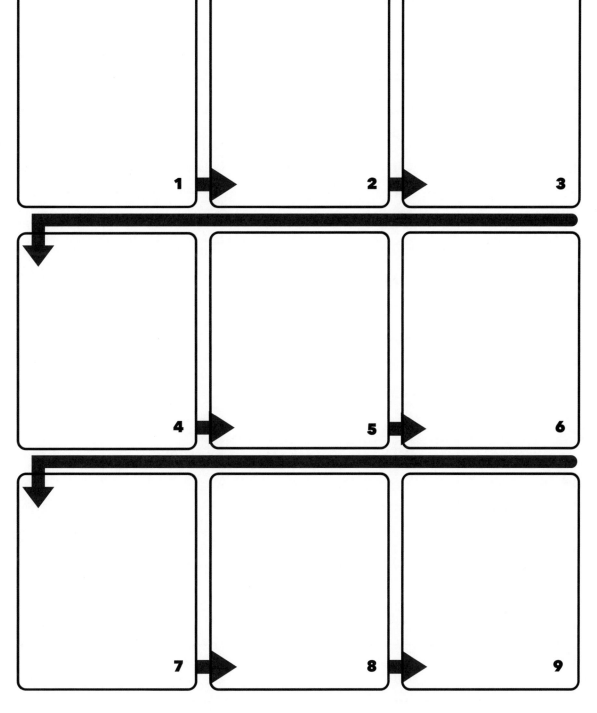

COMMONLY USED PREPOSITIONS

aboard	about	above	across	after
against	along	amid	among	anti
around	as	at	before	behind
below	beneath	beside	besides	between
beyond	but	by	concerning	considering
despite	down	during	except	excepting
excluding	following	for	form	in
inside	into	like	minus	near
of	off	on	onto	opposite
outside	over	past	per	plus
regarding	round	save	since	then
through	to	toward	towards	under
underneath	unlike	until	up	upon
versus	via	with	within	without

You have permission to reproduce this page for use in your classroom.

ENGAGING™
LEARNERS